Nectar of Nondual Truth

CONTENTS

10 Two Key Aspects of Jainism
by Swami Brahmeshananda
How can seemingly contradictory aspects such as austerity and selfless service go together? The answer is that they must, in order that said service be pure of any and all ulterior motive.

16 Truth and Karma
by Annapurna Sarada
What to speak of crucial matters like spiritual growth, even the simple actions and circumstances of everyday life flow in harmony when Truth is maintained. Existence thrives or expires based upon the presence or absence of Truth — in living It and telling it, both.

19 Exploring Gaudapada's Philosophy
by Lex Hixon
The first of a series of classes that Lex Hixon gave on classic Advaita Vedanta is transcribed herein, which scrutinizes the naturally homogenous nature of this most subtle of all philosophical perspectives. To understand Advaita Vedanta is to enter into the most intimate union with Divine Reality and experience that rare authentic spirituality that is scarcely realized otherwise.

27 Vedanta and Today's Youth
by Babaji Bob Kindler
As Swami Vivekananda has stated, *"When will man be friend to man?"* It is within the atmosphere of this fine sentiment and under the inspiration of this prime directive that this article is offered for consideration. For, one of the main reasons that revealed scriptures like the Upanisads and the Bhagavad Gita are still available today, in modern times, free of interpolation and text-torturing, is due to the fact that the heads of families in ancient times passed the torch of such wisdom to their children at an early age. That we are failing to do so in modern times is certainly one of the reasons for the decline of society and humanity.

34 Blessed are the Peacebuilders
by Rev. Canon Charles P. Gibbs
Within the boundless spirit of Universality, the ideal of world Peace is cherished by all lovers of God, and by the sincere well-wishers of humanity.

37 Sacred Sufi Poetry
by Doctor Nahid Angha
In line with the ultimate Goal of all Eastern religions, the sacred poetry of Sufism, along with its composers, declares that only the Beloved is worth seeking. All else falls subservient to "That." Therefore, Kubir sings: *"Dive deep, O mind, dive deep in the Ocean of God's Beauty. If you descend to the uttermost depths, there you will find the gem of Love."*

40 Noncompromise in Advaita Vedanta
by Shivakumar Viswanathan
In an age where both God and higher religious and philosophical ideals are being either cast away completely or heavily compromised, it will benefit the serious seeker of Truth to both see through and resist the tendency to lower the spiritual standard in the least, or, as one poet-saint states: *"Never allow the world's opinion to dim the ecstasy of your worship, or draw you even slightly away from The Mother's sweet intimacy."*

44 Facing Our Fear
by Swami Aseshananda
With the exhortation, *"Be bold, be fearless,"* Swami Vivekananda bolstered the strength of his devotees, East and West, knowing that fear is the worst kind of weakness. In this recently transcribed talk, Swami Aseshananda re-affirms this crucial message.

50 We Are Atman All-Abiding
by Babaji Bob Kindler
Composed in 1995 in honor of Lex Hixon, SRV's founder and inspiration to many aspiring souls.

"The purpose is twofold: first, that religion aligned with philosophy get disseminated and become available to humanity in this trouble-prone day and age; second, that through this divine dispensation, the principle of Universality — the truth of all religions — gets propagated as well."

Publisher's Page

Sarada Ramakrishna Vivekananda – SRV Associations
"Setting the feet of humanity on the path of Universal Truth."

Notes on an Advaitic Journal

At the basis of Advaita as the philosophy of Shankara and his gurus, there is Advaita as experience. Advaita as experience represents that supreme place where all diversity merges in its Essence. It is not combatant or immiscible with qualified or dualistic approaches, but rather provides them their place of consummate arrival. Where actual practice rather than mere book learning is emphasized, where religion, philosophy and spirituality are not separate from one another, where knowledge and love, reason and devotion, are never divorced from each other, there does the truth of authentic nonduality effloresce.

Historically speaking, experiential Advaita originated with the ancient Rishis. Therefore, the Upanisads contain the nondual truths of the Vedas which declare: idam mahabhutam anantam aparam vijnanaghana eva, *"This great Being is endless and without limit. It is a mass of indivisible Consciousness only."*

SRV Associations & Universality

The SRV Associations are part of a worldwide movement of spiritual aspirants devoted to the study and practice of Vedanta and Divine Mother Wisdom. The ideals of this ancient pathway to God, exemplified in the lives of Sri Sarada Devi, Sri Ramakrishna and Swami Vivekananda, are the original and eternal perfection of the Soul and its inherent oneness with Reality, the manifesting of divinity in our lives, selfless service of all beings as God, and reverence for the ultimate unity of all sacred traditions. To this end our purpose is to study, worship, and contemplate Truth so that spirituality may flourish. This is the Advaitic way — *"None else but Self, none other than Mother."*

With reverent gratitude, we heartily thank the contributing writers of this issue of Nectar of Nondual Truth who have so graciously and selflessly shared the wisdom of their respective traditions and practices.

Nectar's Mission — Advaita-Satya-Amritam

In Sanskrit, amrita, nectar also means Immortality – and this is, indeed, what we are offering: opportunities to become aware of this Amrita that is our very Essence via the rarefied teachings from Vedanta and the World Religions and Philosophies that appear in each issue of Nectar.

Nectar of Non-Dual Truth is SRV Associations' heartfelt offering of highest Wisdom to the human community. It is the sincerest form of love and service we know to disseminate non-dual Truth and teachings which transmit pure knowledge, pure love, and true universality. Through Nectar we are working out SRV's mission of spiritual upliftment and education. Please join us; this is a universal movement.

Keeping Nectar in Print

Nectar is a free magazine that can be ordered in printed form online at www.srv.org and also viewed online. However, substantial donations are needed every year to maintain this publication in print. Why is this important?

1 – Printed Nectars are best for person to person and organization to organization dissemination of these ennobling teachings that deepen one's own spiritual life and engender knowledge of, acceptance, and reverence for all other paths.

2 – Only printed copies can reach those who do not have access to online viewing, including prison inmates, who are a particular focus of SRV's social seva.

Use the subscription/donation form provided at the back of this issue to send a check or credit card payment to SRV Associations, P.O. Box 1364, Honokaa, HI., 96727, or donate online at www.srv.org. Your donations are tax deductible.

---

* **Addition/Correction to Nectar Issue #28, 2013**
Quotations from John Cassian in Edward Ulrich's article, "Early Christian Asceticism," were taken from John Cassian: The Conferences, trans. Boniface Ramsey (New York: Paulist Press, 1997). The New Jerusalem Bible was also quoted.

Staff of Nectar of Nondual Truth

Publisher
Sarada Ramakrishna Vivekananda Associations
an Annual Publication
For more information concerning the SRV Associations or Nectar of Nondual Truth please contact:
SRV Associations, PO Box 1364, Honoka'a, HI 96727
Phone: (808) 990-3354
e-mail: srvinfo@srv.org   website: www.srv.org
Nectar Subscription is on a donation basis only

No part of this publication may be reproduced or transmitted in any form without permission from the publisher. Entire contents copyright 2014. All Rights Reserved. ISSN 1531-1414

Editor
Babaji Bob Kindler

Associate Editor
Annapurna Sarada

Production
Lokelani Kindler

Acknowledgement
*Image of Ramakrishna's Disciples
Courtesy of Vedanta Press*
800-816-2242

Cover – Babaji Bob Kindler

Contributing Writers
Swami Aseshananda
Swami Brahmeshananda
Alexander Hixon
Rev. Canon Charles P. Gibbs
Doctor Nahid Angha
Annapurna Sarada
Shivakumar Viswanathan
Babaji Bob Kindler

EDITORIAL

The Great Master Sri Ramakrishna Paramahamsa, said: "God can be realized through all paths. All religions are true. The important thing is to reach the roof. You can reach it by stone stairs or by wooden stairs or by bamboo steps or by a rope. You can also climb up a bamboo pole or jump from a nearby tree. You may say that there are many errors and superstitions in another religion. I should reply: Suppose there are. Every religion has errors. Everyone thinks his own watch alone gives the correct time. It is enough to have yearning for God. It is enough to love Him and feel attracted to Him. Don't you know that God is the inner guide? He sees the longing of our heart and the yearning of our soul."

With this deep yet simple description of the universality of all religions, SRV Associations, under the auspice of its Chosen Ideals, Sri Ramakrishna, Sri Sarada Devi, and Swami Vivekananda, offers its 29th issue of Nectar of Nondual Truth into the world-wide community of truth seekers everywhere. The purpose is twofold: first, that religion aligned with philosophy get disseminated and become available to humanity in this trouble-prone day and age; second, that through this divine dispensation, the principle of Universality — the truth of all religions — gets propagated as well. For, as we often say in SRV Loka, "There is no such thing as a foreign religion; all religions are indigenous to your soul."

To this fine end, then, we are to laud and applaud all Nectar contributors towards this singular principle, writers and spiritual leaders from both different walks of life, and from various traditions as well. They are fine examples of the potential of a people united in a world of beings and societies who only grant lip-service to such high-minded causes, but seldom follow through in action and in realization. As Swami Vivekananda has pleaded, "When will man finally be friend to man?"

Everyone who is familiar with the New Age's several decade romance with interreligious forums has seen that putting a selection of religious leaders from different traditions together in the same room for a spiritual caucus offers no profound solution; it has not solved anything yet. About the only thing that has been settled is that we must learn to "agree to disagree." What is really wanted are those unique individuals who, after having gained enlightenment along the pathway they have chosen to tread, are then able to escape the limitations of all religious perspectives, at least temporarily, and minister to the dispensation of what our SRV founder, Lex Hixon, called "the wide open space beyond all religions." This task cannot be accomplished by either forsaking all religions, or by sticking narrowly to our own; rather, it will require that we study all scriptures, understand the intrinsic oneness of their founders (like Abraham, Moses, Jesus, and Mohammed), know all religions and then warmly and openly frequent both the people and the communities that hold and practice them. To quote Swami Vivekananda on this selfsame subject:

"What is India, or England, or America to us? We are the servants of that God who by the ignorant is called man. He who pours water at the root, does he not water the whole tree? We want to lead humanity to the place where there is neither the Vedas, the Bible, nor the Koran; yet this has to be done by harmonizing the Vedas, Bible, and Koran. Let some of you spread like wildfire, and preach the worship of the universal aspect of God — a thing that has never been undertaken before in our country. No quarreling with people, we must be friends with all."

It is with this ideal in mind that the pages of this truth-journal can be opened, and the nectar that abides therein shall be ingested, comprehended, and doled out to all beings. As Shankara states about this Nondual Truth: "For those who are suffering from the effects of the sun's rays on the road of this world, the cool water of Advaita (nonduality) will reveal the presence of Brahman."
Peace, Peace, Peace.
Babaji Bob Kindler

NECTAR OF ADVAITIC INSTRUCTION

Questions from Our Readers

The invaluable practice of Atma-vichara (intricate questioning as to the nature of Reality) continues, acting as the firm basis for spiritual ascension in Vedantic circles, and in all religious traditions, each in their own way.

General Vedantic Subjects

"Why is it that one can practice viveka, discrimination between the real and the unreal, can see the distinction between the changing and the unchanging, and still cannot detach from the changing?"

This is at once a good question, an astute observation, and a frustrating development. Why indeed? It is, in part, because of attachment to the unreal, which persists in the mind until either satiation or renunciation removes it forever. Further, satiation will only occur under the auspices of the dharma, and not otherwise. Without adherence and fealty to the dharma, desires in the mind will only ignite further, not disperse.

The solution for this contrary situation is matured spiritual practice gotten via longevity along the path. Greater and deeper experiences need to be had. Comprehension of the need for viveka is an excellent beginning; it only requires deepening through vairagya. Vairagya has some twelve stages to it according to the tradition. As one practices it, the Six Jewels — Shatsampati, accrue. Soon, all that changes will not bother the aspirant anymore. It is all a matter of follow through.

"I don't understand the statement from the Upanisads that 'the soul is divided and subdivided hundreds of times.' Can you explain this?"

Here, we utilize the word, "apparent," in order to explain. The undivided Soul "appears" to divide. That it does so is really a false superimposition, vivarta. In other words, this is a qualified nondual teaching, not a nondual one. The seers make provisions for people's differing levels of understanding by using such statements in the scriptures. It helps beings to comprehend life and mind. Notice that the word, "soul," is lower-cased. That means the mind, not the Atman. The mind in Vedanta is what moves, travels, transmigrates. Soul, upper-cased, means Atman; It is ever-stationary and all-pervasive.

The richness of qualified nondualism comes in here as well. The explanation of the subdivision process really lends both credence and beauty to life in the Cosmos. It implies a network of subtle nadis, an infinite array of nerve-channels, along which transmigrating souls (minds in mental projection mode) pass to and fro, coming and going in a stream of consciousness that projects itself here and there, as in a series of dreams. So much is accounted for in such a description, and many age-old questions get answered. The furthest step, the highest plateau, called Nonduality, is thus made easier of comprehension as well.

"In *Karma Yoga*, Swamiji mentions the power of words and how if person A insults person B, and B gets angry, he does so because his mind was in such a state as to be receptive to the insult spoken by A. Does this imply that if B gets angry or violent at words spoken by A, it is as much B's fault as it is A's? Is getting angry or violent in response to insults or words a choice? It seems that part of practicing nonviolence in thought is keeping the mind in a state that is non-receptive to the insults and violent words of others, like water running down a stone wall. Is my application of this teaching of nonviolence correct? And it seems that conventional correctness goes out the door with this teaching, because if I am a careful practitioner of nonviolence in thought, word, and deed, and someone gets offended by my actions, I do not need to brood on the fact that they got irritated."

About persons A and B, yes, it is a fact that the entire outcome rests in the mind of the more wise of the two, the more nonviolent of the two minds. It would be mere morality to think in terms of who is right and who is wrong, since the worldly are always "in the wrong" but do not know it yet. And it would also be mere defensive thinking to assume that I have to protect myself from evil and injustice for the sake of some vaunted attitude of pride and victory. Plainly put, the spiritual person removes all traces of negativity from the mind, so that when injustice and hatred, etc., visit themselves upon his life, he does not react. That is, if "beauty is in the eye of the beholder," so must evil and hatred be there as well. That is why we attempt to *"Resist not evil."* Christ did not free the adulteress from a stoning because he wanted to save her, or because he had compassion: these are evident and natural in a realized soul. He did so because he could not see imperfection in her. Put Vedantically, she was Atman, not human.

And so we free our minds from colorations, from sublations, from projections, from past conditionings, and attain Freedom Itself. Then we turn to see That perfection everywhere, and we are then, and not before, the best "helpers" of humanity.

"Where can I find a good resource for studying the Eight Limbs of Yoga, especially the Yamas and Niyamas? I continue to struggle with understanding several of these. I could ask about several of these individually, but think I should read about them first. Is it imperative that I have a deep understanding of the first two limbs before proceeding further with the Raja Yoga lessons?"

The Raja Yoga email lessons that you are receiving will take you through the first two limbs of Yoga soon enough, and the commentators for this email class — Vedavyasa, Vivekananda, and yours truly — will flesh out the teachings of the yamas and niyamas thoroughly. For, to answer your question here, it is best if one really secures mastery over the yamas and niyamas of Yoga before moving on to asana and pranayama, what to speak of meditation and the bid for Samadhi. And, in fact, part of the reason that beginning aspirants fall off of the razor's-edged path is due to not spending time in these prerequisites. In other words, imagine the folly of those minds who think they can master the seated posture (asana) without first attaining nonviolence (ahimsa) and noncovetousness (asteya). Do they think they can sit still and focus before they have mastered the mind's tendency to engage in violent actions? And just think of the delusion present in the mind of that immature and reactive beginner who presumes that he or she can meditate (dhyana) on the Absolute, even on the cosmic process within (like the succession of alambanas), without first attaining a little inner strength by austerity (tapas), some inner peace (santosha), and studying and committing to memory the words of the seers and past masters (svadhyaya). And do they think that they can plumb the depths of limitless Consciousness devoid of devotion to those singular friends in high places (Ishvara-pranidhana)?

So the answer here is a definitive "yes," and thank you for bringing it up again. The yamas and niyamas are to be mastered first, for if they are not, then spiritual life lasts all but a few months — as is seen by the hosts of beings who are moving in, then out, of the monastery, ashrams, and spiritual sanghas all of the time. For the most part it is a march of fools. For the qualified aspirant, however, well-schooled and well-guided, Vivekananda states that one should be able to become a practiced yogi in six months! Simply remain devoted and constant to guru, dharma, and sangha. Otherwise you only send a wrong message to your society, your children, and your own mind.

"If one watches movies that have violent or sexually explicit content, is this going to deepen the samskaras that drive unchecked/unhealthy/distracting appetites for sex and violence? Whether it be an appetite for sex/violence in real life or to see it on TV makes no difference for the spiritual aspirant. In other words, like my mother used to say, 'Garbage in, garbage out' is true in all aspects of life. The spiritual aspirant wants to always put God in, in order to get God out."

As far as violent movies, etc., yes, it all depends on the quality of one's consciousness. For the worldly, they will only pour gas on the fire of desire. For the luminary, it does not matter what they see or sense, as their minds and senses are always under their control. For the aspirant, however, it will matter sometimes, other times not so much. That is, when the mind is sattvic and it witnesses violence, there will be no impression or residue left on it. When in rajas or tamas, though, the corresponding element will arise and leave its similar impression.

Role of Food in Spiritual Life

"What regulations of food are to be observed when one takes up Raja Yoga (and Yoga in general)? I would assume there is some correlation here with the sattvic food described by Sri Krishna in the later chapters of the Gita? Have there been any illumined beings who have mentioned individual constitution playing a role in food regulation?"

In response to your final question first, the luminaries seldom, if ever, talk about food; the scriptures, almost never. It is really for the individual to work out. Certainly, issues like sensitivity to nature, nonviolence against animals, and the like, will be considered, especially given the crassness and almost brutish, certainly callous, behavior of humanity in this day and times. Once individual health is attained, one can verily make a statement for positive change by the way one conducts oneself in the face of society's insensitivity. For instance, I doubt there are very many people/bodies that really "need" red meat; they just think they do. Often times, for those who do not have the strength of raw austerity in them, adding fish — the "vegetables of the sea" — into the diet, will be enough. I personally cannot fathom consuming seared dead birds, but I suppose that has to be listed as an option for those with a still strong desire for flesh eating.

Definitely, you may study the particulars of this subject in the Gita, specifically in its three forms — the Gunas. Basically, follow the sattvic way there. In addition, and as I have said before, read all about the role of food in the book, *Reclaiming Kundalini Yoga*, where I have put it as succinctly as possible.

Generally speaking, now, I can say that most of us in the early days of our sadhana turned vegetarian in our twenties, and gave up eating certain foods like meat, onions, garlic, etc. That we also gave up the poor eating habits of our parents goes without saying, i.e., white flour, white sugar, overly processed foods, many sweets except for honey and the like. While cutting out those two categories of questionable foods, we sustained ourselves with a mass of vegetables, grains like brown rice, tofu and veggie proteins, fruits, nuts, beans, and generally anything from the organic garden that was wholesome.

Having said that, I can say that some of my generation who became sensitive to food issues had to modify further according to physique as well, and also due to certain issues like allergies, problems with dairy, etc. Moreover, once we had adapted and changed what was seen as a normal diet in those earlier days, we eventually found we could go back to some of those foodstuffs without problems. Some took to meat-eating again, but with a different mindset and a totally new way of evaluating meat — what to speak of moderating it — like giving up red meat, for instance. An experimental phase was thus helpful in finding what worked for each personal constitution. For myself, it was joyful vegetarianism all the way, never looking back or needing to, but keeping some dairy in the diet for substance.

Finally, there should be nothing of the moral level superimposed on this area. We cannot, for instance, insist that the Eskimo live on vegetables in the northernmost climes of the world just because meat-eating is considered bad. What would they find in the frozen waste to eat? Iceberg lettuce? Snow peas? Once, some fish found its way to the lunch table at my guru's ashram. This was a rare occurrence, but devotees sometimes brought in food from their homes as offerings. One new woman devotee was shocked that afternoon, and stood up yelling, "There's a dead fish on the table!" My guru appeared at the doorway of the dining room and stated firmly, "The Atman never dies!" Such is the real point of the matter, which is precisely why the seers and the scriptures do not bring the subject of food into spiritual life. We are transcending the physical when we engage in seeking God, and certainly when we meditate. Why stymie the inward moving consciousness by constantly obsessing with what one puts in the stomach? Just do everything mindfully, knowing that Consciousness is indestructible.

Meditation

"Can meditation times be kept spontaneous when worldly duties and schedule allow? For example, the last three days it has felt almost effortless to meditate upon first awakening. Thus, I've meditated at 3:30 am, and between 5 and 6:30."

It is not so much that meditation "can be" kept spontaneous, but that in this day and age it is often that it "has to be"; people are just too busy, and at the beck and call of the world and its activities and allurements, to have it any other way. Only rare souls paddle up stream. Ordinary souls float easily downstream on their pleasure crafts, finally entering the ocean of Samsara. So, like the paths themselves, the fruits of these two ways are entirely different in nature.

To meditate effortlessly is often a case of the gunas being balanced (sattva in predominance) and one's karmas being temporarily in abeyance. All that will pass, unfortunately, and one will be up against it all a few days later, struggling to keep spiritual life alive and well in the world. So, in this case, it is better to adhere to a regimen and never let it go, doing it regularly, the same time of day and night, without deviation. In other words, since one never knows when the mind will change, and when negativities will come one's way, it is best to always keep up the defensive and aggressive posture of practice. This pertains to formal practice, not to spontaneity. In the case of the latter, one can sit anytime one wants (so long as the formal sitting has been accomplished), and be spontaneous at all other times (excepting when formal practice is warranted). This is the best way to advance spiritually. All other ways leave things to "chance."

"Regarding meditation with form, I've done the 15-20 minutes of meditation on my Ishtam with the preinitiation mantra everyday, followed by 15-20 minutes of formless meditation as instructed. Can I meditate on other forms if I want to after mantra practice? Can I meditate on Sri Krishna, or the Guru, or the image of Swamiji and one of his disciples? Can I also meditate on a teaching to try to get further perspective, perhaps by repeating a sloka over and over again in meditation?"

Yes, and like the answer to the above question, after formal practice has been carried out to the letter, then is the time of general meditation and contemplation — like reflection on the scriptures taught by the guru and thinking over the lives of the realized souls via their images and teachings. All of this leads to a well-rounded spiritual practice, and will result — if kept constant — in the "death of ignorance."

Rebirth/Reincarnation

"I'm still pondering what you mean by the soul straying from the true path and taking embodiment in space and time, that being a primal error. What choices would the SOUL have if it didn't individualize itself? How does it get temporarily disoriented? What is the true path before embodiment?"

So long as the transmigrating soul's karmas remained unresolved, the true path before embodiment is identical with the path after embodiment; they cannot be separated. From the realms of the ancestors, or from lower and higher heavenly states and back to earth, the soul moves, as if in a dream, not knowing the reasons why it constantly projects itself. Its true nature, Atman (SOUL, as you write it here), is ever-stationary and does not move about. One needs to prove this to oneself via rapt and still meditation. As Vivekananda has stated, this coming and going is all nonsense. To read it in his own words: *"Coming and going is all pure delusion. The Soul never comes nor goes. Where is the place to which it shall go, when all of space is in the Soul? When shall be the time of entering or departing, when all of time is in the Soul?"* This statement is profound, and the real essence of Advaita Vedanta. It imparts to us, and from the lips of a rare, illumined soul, both the mechanics of maya and the truth of Nonduality — as he said, *"The truth of 'All is Brahman.'"*

In other words, then, and to address the first part of your question, the real path of the Soul is no path at all. All pathways lie within the dreaming mind, where nature and maya exist. The Goal *Is* the Soul, but not the transmigrating one (the mental complex). To travel from realm to realm is to move from one dream to another, and everything associated with such movement lies in Maya. As Gaudapada counsels us in his famous karika, *"A runner running a race in a dream goes nowhere."* On the other side of the equation, Ramprasad sings in one of his wisdom songs: *"To be born in this body composed of earth is a heavy burden for the soaring Soul. To incarnate again and again across the face of this vast planetary realm can never slake our burning thirst. The poor one who sings this song proclaims: 'No more birth for me from the womb of matter, only emanation from my Divine Mother.'"*

Now, another thing may be mentioned here, which may possibly be more to the point of your query. A fully conscious incarnation, called a divine life, is also true. Fully aware beings accomplish this when they embody. The only thing about this — and all the wise luminaries say so — is that such a "birth" cannot be classed as a birth at all, since the Essence of the Soul, Atman, is neither forgotten nor strayed away from in the least. In other words, a divine life is existence lived in Self-realization. It has nothing to do with seeking or finding; it has no karma to answer for. Delusion, suffering, dreaming, searching, or living for the purposes of mere enjoyment, are not found in It, are alien to It. It is not birth at all, then, as the song above explains, but only "emanation." An emanation never disconnects from the Source it emits from, say, like dreaming does, for if it did, that pure ray of light would simply dissolve in space and time, in Maya. And actually, this is what taking birth, life, and death in Maya is like, what it is all about. It is *"running a race in a dream."* Beings may look back and think that they have made progress, gained substance, and actually went somewhere. But there is nowhere to go in a realm consisting of illusion. A hamster running constantly on an exercise wheel in a cage fails to move even an inch.

There is no way to make Maya work for oneself. *"It is nei-

ther real, nor unreal, nor neither, nor a combination of both." And, as Sri Ramakrishna has said, *"Never study Maya; observe it from a distance."* If one studies it, like, for instance, physics and science are doing, it only sweeps one into it. Soon, one is beholding the particles of one's universe to be changing at a billionth of a second, and as a result getting hypnotized to such an extent that one cannot conclude that it is all Maya, that it and its objects are empty — that the world is ephemeral, like all the true luminaries of the past have told us. It cannot be owned, it cannot fulfill, and the fact that even intelligent beings seek to possess and gain satisfaction from such emptiness (shunyata) is the real definition of delusion here on earth.

The question may be asked, then: what constitutes the realization of an illumined soul who "emanates" bodies devoid of mayic delusion? The answer? That selfsame renunciation of all things temporal, or all things changing, of the entire empirical process. And there is another facet to his realization as well. He knows that 1) all phenomena have proceeded from the mental process, and 2) that it all exists within him, not outside. *"All is Brahman."* To the realized soul, the world is Brahman. To the bound soul seeking freedom, the world eventually reveals itself as Maya. To the one-sided intellectual devoid of spiritual wisdom and proper discrimination, the world is falsely taken to be real. To the worldly person seeking pleasure and fulfillment, the world is his or her oyster, but lost in a sea of temporality and empty appearances. To the lost soul, the world is a prison house of suffering. To most beings here on earth, they do not care one way or another. They only practice the "Yoga of Apathy."

Back to the final aspect of your question, unless one sees and knows the Formless Essence underlying all manifestation, all expression, and all appearances, form may as well *Be* delusion. Taking a form would then constitute bondage. Venturing into *"the realms of name and form in time and space based upon cause and effect"* (Vivekananda's definition of Maya) would then epitomize disorientation. Such pointless wandering creates desires that are both connected to and a product of the soul's original desire to embody apart from or devoid of the knowledge of Brahman. Here, that familiar adage, "....don't leave home without it," pertains perfectly to the soul's exit from Formless Reality, and its entrance into the realms of name and form. As Vivekananda has put it, when asked if a man should embody: *"I certainly hope he will not; not until he can do so in full Consciousness."*

Mental Projection

"Can you please give a concrete example of how to see something is a projection of the mind? How can I see the cup of tea I drink is a projection of the mind? Is it that I think, 'I'll have a cup of tea,' and then proceed to get one? But even then, the tea is traced back to the bag and the hot water. Then, those materials are traced back to the plants and the materials from which they came. So then, is it that nature itself was projected out of the mind?"

When you think that you will have a cup of tea, that is only simple desire. But the cup and the tea/water themselves have come out of the mind because matter has come from the mind, and cup and tea are matter, are they not? So yes, when inspected deeply one finds — all the seers and yogis and luminaries have found — that all of matter, of nature, is within them. We hear that saying quite often in different forms, like *"Everything is within you,"* and *"The kingdom of heaven is within you."* In the All-Creating King Tantra, Samantrabadra put it, *"The root of all beings and things is nothing else but one Self. I am that place in which all existence resides."* We accept this or not, according to the quality of our faith. But of those who accept this, few connect their agreement of this teaching to the actual dynamics of manifestation. To do so would be to know that all of nature is in the mind first in the form of thoughts, all of those based in Intelligence. The difficulty for most beings, however, after they have acceded to this fact, is to comprehend that the mind "projects" forms; it does not "create" them. If things could actually be created, they could also be destroyed, but we never see such destruction! Yes, we see it momentarily, but who has seen an end to existence yet, on any level? Even to the materialist, when man is gone, the universe is still here. It all just keeps going, reproducing, cycling, reincarnating, and this pertains to everything — matter, nature, worlds, living beings, thoughts, intelligence, deities — it is all Eternal. And certainly God, Brahman, is Eternal, Imperishable. And that is why all else is so. There is no such thing as a "created" thing, then. One cannot create something out of nothing. One cannot produce a thing that is unproduced in its very essence, by its very nature.

To borrow a page from Gaudapada's Karika: *"A real creation is an impossibility. When a thing is produced, that means it was unproduced before. In other words, its nature (before) was to be unproduced. A thing cannot change its nature. An unproduced thing must remain unproduced. Thus, the so-called production of a thing is only due to Maya, is never actual. If production were real, it would be like saying that an already produced thing is being produced. In the case of a nonexistent thing, it is obvious that it cannot be produced either in reality or through Maya. So, the mind vibrates in dream to produce false objects, and in the waking state it does the same; yet the real Mind remains nondual throughout. Duality, then, is brought about by mind-vibration. The true Mind enjoys Samadhi of Brahman all the time. Mind in deep sleep is under the spell of ignorance, and at that time has its tendencies only lying dormant."*

Thus, objects being projections of the mind, are empty; all forms are empty — shunya. For example, a projection, say, like on a screen in a movie, is a passing phenomenon. All that happens in a movie causes no effect on the screen. There are no rips on the screen from explosions, there is no wetness on the screen from tears cried, and there certainly is no leftover impression in any way on the screen after the movie is over. That is because the phenomena projected have no real substance of their own. Yet, it is still there, all of it, imprinted on the film stored in the canister up on the shelf in the projection booth. Cosmic Mind with its unmanifested prakriti is that booth and its shelf, like a chest of drawers owned by the Divine Mother of the Universe. She pulls "thought-things" out of it and makes them available as gross objects, and after they are used, they get properly washed, ironed, folded, and returned to their respective drawers.

There is your example, then. To summate:
1) All objects are made of concretized thought.
2) Thus, these objects are projections of Mind.

3) Further, these objects are never created, but are only ideas projected from their unmanifested state that have taken form by solidifying in the manifested state.

4) Objects are empty of abiding substance, i.e., ever-changing, which is why they appear and disappear over many cycles, and can never be grasped, owned, known, or truly enjoyed.

5) Being unreal, they are nevertheless indestructible, having their source in a formless state.

"I've begun to inspect my thoughts using witness consciousness. It has been helpful to know I can discard the bad ones and other garbage that gets into my mind. What I would like to know is, how do I begin to trace them back to their origin so that I may destroy the source of the bad thoughts?"

"Destroying" thoughts is not possible, what to speak of their source. Rather, one returns them to the curtain of cosmic ignorance from which they sprang. Mind, at all three levels, consists of thoughts and their power, called Chitta. And "Chit happens," as we say. A perfectly still mind, well, how many have attained that? But to start, one can practice controlling thoughts so that they do not rise up when they are not wanted, and insinuate themselves on life situations — especially at the most undesirable times. Or, to put it in a more positive way, that thoughts only come when you want them, to assist you, inspire you, etc.

Therefore, knowing this fact first (so that one does not try and proceed under the false assumption that thoughts can be destroyed), the subject of tracing origins comes up. And it is precisely the exercise of tracing origins that helps one to realize that nothing is ever destroyed, for when one finds the origin — of matter, of worlds, of thoughts, of intelligence — one finds that actual creation is a myth, an impossibility. Simply put, everything exists at all times. It is just a matter of whether it is in a manifested or unmanifested state in any given period of time. To actually bring anything, like objects, worlds, bodies, intelligence, especially a soul — The Soul — into being from nothingness, is absurd, is the thinking of addled brains.

Speaking of origins, where did such odd misconceptions such as creation out of nothing come from? Why is it that so few have discovered the simple truth that everything is a projection of the mind? As the Prajnaparamita Sutra states it, *"The Sutra of the Diamond Cutter of Supreme Wisdom declares that all phenomena are projections of one's own mind. The work of cutting away mental conceptualization brings one to the furthest shore of Enlightenment."* In the Mahamudra teaching of Tibet, it gets expressed in this way: *"All manifestation, the Universe itself, is contained in the mind, and the true nature of mind is the realm of illumination, shining with radiance that can neither be conceived or touched."*

This is what you are on the trail of, that we are calling "inspecting one's own consciousness." Did you think that the purpose is only to rid oneself of negative thoughts? They never should have been there in the first place! It is ignoble for anyone to entertain them. It is most unfortunate that a spiritually realized soul, who has spent a dedicated series of lifetimes realizing the Highest Truth, has to come to earth and take so much time helping people rid their minds of contents that have no business being there in the first place, and all that effort before the luminary can introduce to them precepts like Projectionism over the Creation Theory. As the poet wrote, *"Grasping matter, losing Grace, strange indeed this human race."*

Watching, in order, with a single eye, Intelligence emanating off of The Word, thoughts radiating from Intelligence, gradated worlds formulating from the collective thoughts of the multitudes (deities, celestials, human beings, etc.), and finally, objects congealing due to the (solidifying, liquefying) power residing in the mind and senses, the newborn seer's previously held beliefs around creation theories and evolution get replaced by the stunning insight that everything is a projection, not a creation. And Mind is the projector. Matter does not have any intelligence to do this with. All matter can do is congeal and dissolve at the behest of the power of intelligence.

Certainly, this is a much deeper answer to your simple question than you expected, but imagine the fate of negative thoughts under the power of such a revelation! Would they dare even rise up anymore, once such profundity had visited the mind? Conventional persons talk glibly about the power of positive thinking: but what about the power of higher thinking leading to no thinking at all? This is uncharted territory for most beings. The seer can rid himself of all thoughts — positive, negative, mixed, superficial — anytime he wants to, and then enjoy pure, conscious Awareness. There is no mind There to bother him; only the mind's Nondual Origin. It is Samadhi. Personality may be gone, or placed in abeyance for a time, but that does not leave only an insentient void as some suspect and fear, like "emptiness"; not unless one defines "emptiness" as empty of problems, empty of brooding, empty of suffering, empty of impeding forms, empty of nagging ego and its hosts of names and desires — and particularly, empty of binding concepts.

In short, tracing origins leads the soul to That which is beyond all origins — Brahman, Allah, All-Mighty Father. That is an Ocean of Existence, Knowledge, and Bliss Absolute. Glimpsing That, the human soul will no longer think of anything else but That. What happens to thoughts then?

"Can you explain the difference between 'dull mind' and 'no mind?' How would the mindset of a person be different towards, say, work, for example, who has a dull mind versus having no mind? Perhaps this is a silly question. I'm trying to understand the practicality of these different modes of the states of the mind."

It is a silly question; then it is not. The reason for this is the "look-alike" quality of tamas and sattva. Dull mind and sattvic mind appear similar from the outside; that is, that both modes are rather inactive. But do not let that fool you. There is much going on inside the sattvic mind. Plans for the highest good of oneself and others are percolating there. This is not true of the dull mind, however, which is only lethargic.

And what to speak of sattvic mind, you are citing "no mind" here! That is an animal of an entirely different color altogether; it is actually colorless. We cannot assess "no mind." It is advaita, nondualism, in action....or, in inaction, really. One can only "apprentice" That in the company of one who is a past master of It. Then It will "rub off" on you over time. It is the reason that most beings take to spiritual life in the first place, whether they know it at the time or not; most do not.

You see, a young man once went to a guru to get instructions. His mind was heavy with fear, brooding, worldly thoughts, restlessness, and the like. The master only had him take teachings and meditate for a time in his presence. A few days later the man left with a buoyant mind, free of heaviness. What really got transmitted there and then was "no mind." People tend to think of it as a void, as emptiness, but if they do, they are completely clueless about it. It is empty alright — empty of all the things which plague mankind's thinking process. When these are removed he can enjoy again his own pristine Awareness. Come to find, as well, that when he engages in action thereafter, it is 1) free of karmic repercussion and, 2) highly beneficial to those around him. What a simple wonder! As my teacher used to quip, *"No mind, no matter. No matter, never mind."*

Jnana Matra, The Intelligent Particle

"In reviewing the SRV live-streaming classes, in the Jnana Matra series and its main chart, why are the Jnana Matras called intelligence particles? Is it because the fundamental intelligence operates through or by them? When I contemplate the chart, I see all existence in them, as if in seed form, and think, Why aren't they called something like "being units," or "possibility," or "probability," or "seeds of existence?" But instead, the word 'intelligence' is used. Why?"

It has to do with knowledge and wisdom, at least from the standpoint of the embodied soul. From the higher perspective, like the realm of the luminaries, they perceive Intelligence as the first principle out of the gate at the time of Cosmic Projection. Intelligence is closely akin to Consciousness; almost identical. As Vivekananda has stated, mixed in with other teachings:

"Though knowledge, being a compound, cannot be the Absolute itself, it is the nearest approach to it, and higher than vasana, will or desire, conscious or unconscious. The Divine first becomes the mixture of knowledge; then, in the second degree, that of will. It is said that plants have no consciousness, that they are at best only unconscious wills; the answer is that even this unconscious plant will is a manifestation of consciousness, not of the plant, but of the Cosmos, the Mahat of Sankhya Philosophy. The Buddhist analysis of everything into will is imperfect, firstly, because will itself is a compound, and secondly, because consciousness or knowledge, which is a compound of the first degree, precedes it. Knowledge is action. First action, then reaction. When the mind perceives, then as the reaction it wills. The will is in the mind. So it is absurd to say that will is the last analysis. Deussen is playing into the hands of the Darwinists."

He states that the Divine first "becomes" knowledge. It thus emanates from pure "Being." He also brings in the Cosmic Mind. Meditate on that Mind as a profound alambana, and you will see that it can be little else if it is not pure Knowledge.

"With regards to your Jnana Matra teaching, and its correlation to the Five Akashas of our tradition, what happens as one moves down the akashas and their corresponding particles? I mean, what drops out from the particles at each lower level? What drops out of the chittakasha? Or to put it another way for the sake of clarity, what is the chittamatra lacking in, that the jnanamatra is not lacking in? And, so on down to the pranamatra and bhutamatra?"

It is good to go both directions when trying to fathom the vibrating particles and the akashas that are formed of them. Along your line of thinking and questioning, then, what gets lost or "drops out" is an interesting way of putting it. One way of saying it, is that subtlety gets lost, while density naturally increases. Consider, for instance, how dense both mind and matter are at the physical world (bhutakasha). As Ramprasad Sen puts it in one of his divine songs, *"To be born in this body composed of earth is a heavy burden for the soaring soul. To incarnate again and again across the face of this vast planetary realm can never slake the thirst of this unique winged creature, who desires to drink water only from the skies, and never from earthly brooks and streams."*

Thus, consciousness and intelligence, the two main ingredients of the Chidakasha and the Jnanakasha, get superimposed over by denser particles, grosser worlds. It would be wrong to assume that they actually get modified in any way, or dumbed down, but it certainly seems that way from the level of physical awareness. A study of the Intelligent Particle (on the chart) will provide a good rendering of what is inherent and eternal — not in the Jnanamatra only, but in all of existence.

To explain further, and taking an example, the seers say that prana is insentient, does not have consciousness and a will of its own. In other words, it is not God, though beings like shamans, occultists, and metaphysicians try hard to make it God. What can be said? It is their version of Atman, as Gaudapada states. But we will put that aside for the moment. Even though it is vibrating with life force, one could say that the particle of prana is missing that essential ingredient that makes for a more pure sentiency — what the seers call Awareness. Prana can carry energy and thoughts, can conduct vital functions, etc., but it is devoid of the singular power of the independent Knower that can be so intuited and cognized in the Intelligent Particle.

A case can be made for what is missing in the grosser particle realms as well, for all of them are subservient to Intelligence. You ask about the chitmatra and its thought realm, as compared to the Jnanakasha. Simply put, all beings have thoughts, but not all are intelligent ones. In fact, precious few of them are. The instinctual thoughts of animals, the evil thoughts of tyrants, the self-serving thoughts of the worldly, the secular thoughts of the intellectuals — and on inwards to the ambitious thoughts of the asuras and the heavenly thoughts of the celestials — all are more or less devoid of any conscious higher Intelligence. Conscious Intelligence is it, then. Inspiration, ingenuity, spiritual awakening, the revelation of scripture, philosophical study and its achievements, spiritual practice and its success — all are indications of the actual presence of Brahman, God. Even such attributes as contentment, peace, and bliss are preeminent qualities of Intelligence. As Vivekananda puts it, *"Where flows the stream [of particles] of knowledge, truth, and the bliss that follows both...."*

Stream of Consciousness, then, conscious thoughts of living Awareness served by all other flows and collections of particles, right on down to the atomic level, is what we are seeing and feeling all the time, and this experience, consciously met and digested, is how we find out the truth of "All is Brahman."

Questions, observations and insights regarding the issues of the day or problems in spiritual life may be directed to Nectar's editorial staff at srvinfo@srv.org and will be duly addressed in succeeding issues.

◆ *Swami Brahmeshananda*

TWO KEY ASPECTS OF JAINISM
AUSTERITY & SERVICE
IN THE WORLD'S MOST NONVIOLENT RELIGION

On the last *Akshaya Tritiya*, a day auspicious to Hindus as well as Jains, I happened to be at Limbdi, a small town in Gujarat, where there is a large community of Jains. I was asked to attend the "fast-breaking ceremony of the year-long-fast" of one of the relatives of a Jain devotee of the local Ramakrishna Ashrama. The person concerned was a young lady, about 25, who had undertaken *varshitapa*, which involves fasting on alternate days and on intervening auspicious days for one year starting from and ending on Akshaya Tritiya. The occasion of the successful completion of the penance was being celebrated with great joy and festivity. The lady was attired in her best dress and was decked from head to foot with gold ornaments. As a sign of recognition and appreciation, every visitor offered a spoonful of sugarcane juice in a small cup for her to drink. Even this kind of participation is considered highly meritorious. Embroidered pictures depicting this scene can often be seen in Jain temples.

Although all the major religions of the world lay stress on austerity (*tapas*) as a means of emancipation, the above description shows what high honor is given in Jainism to a person undertaking tapas. As a matter of fact, so great a stress is laid on tapas in Jainism that it is included as the fourth essential means of salvation, along with the *triratna* of Jainism, viz., right faith, right knowledge, and right conduct. According to Jain philosophy, the individual soul is inherently pure, conscious, blissful, omniscient, and omnipotent, but owing to past karmas its inherent perfection is concealed. The task before the aspirant is to prevent the accumulation of new karmas (*samvara*) and to remove the already accumulated ones (*nirjara*). To the extent the karmic covering is made thinner, the light of the soul shines forth. This nirjara is achieved mainly by tapas. As scripture relates: "*As a large tank, when its supply of water has been stopped, gradually dries up via consumption and evaporation, so also the karmas of a monk, which he has acquired over crores of births, are annihilated by austerities, especially if there be no influx of bad karmas.*" Also, "*He who practices penance and is able to keep his vows, acquires knowledge of scriptures, and becomes capable of controlling the axle of the chariot of meditation.*"

Definition of Tapas in Jainism

Tapas is variously defined by Jain *acharyas*. According to Acharya Malayagiri, that which burns eight types of karma is tapas. Karma is often compared to dry wood, or straw, in Jainism, and hence this derivative meaning is quite apt. Jinadasagani Mahatma also gives a similar derivative meaning, but adds sin (*papa*) with karma. However, Acharya Abhayadevsuri extends the meaning to include emaciation and drying up of the body as well. Another acharya has given an entirely different definition: "*Control of one's desires is tapas.*" According to Acharya Sonabhadra, restraint of senses and the mind is tapas. Summarizing these various views, Pandit Sukhalji says: "*With a view to developing spiritual power adequate for reducing passions, whatever means are adopted for placing one's body, senses, and mind, under purifying hardship, that is called tapas or true penance.*"

As has been pointed out, the main purpose of tapas is the expiation of karmas. However, austerities concentrate the mental energies and strengthen the will-power as well, which may be utilized for fulfillment of desires here and hereafter. Tapas may also impart occult powers to the aspirant, but such *sakama* austerities for ulterior motives, or for name and fame, have been denounced in the ancient Jain scriptures in no uncertain terms.

Tapas in Jainism has been divided into two types: external (*bahiranga*); and internal (*antaranga*). Each of these has six subdivisions. Those austerities which can be seen by others, which are mainly physical and concerned with external observances, are included under external tapas. Those which cannot be seen by others, which are predominantly mental and independent of external aids, are called internal tapas.

External Tapas

(1) Fasting (*anashana*). Religious people often undertake prolonged and extremely rigorous fasts without deriving much spiritual benefit. Such fasting is often denounced by the Gita as tamasic austerity. However, the fact is that fasting is advocated in almost all religions of the world as an important method of mortification. All religions have produced saints who have practiced severe austerities involving fasting. According to Hindu mythology, goddess Parvati did severe tapas in which she gave up eating even the leaves fallen from trees. Lakshmana is believed to have fasted for fourteen years while serving Rama during the years of banishment. These two mythological examples exemplify the Hindu view on fasting. Jesus Christ fasted for forty days; so did Saint Francis of Assisi. The Tibetan saint Milarepa and the Jain prophet Mahavir fasted more often than they took food. Even Sufi saints like Rabia, Baiyazid, and Junaid, often undertook fasts lasting many days. These cases demonstrate the intense desire of humans to achieve conquest over the animal propensities of the body. In other cases, the inspired mind of the person was totally absorbed in the contemplation of something sublime or so engrossed in the devoted service of God that food was altogether forgotten.

Other than the expiation of karmas, the other objectives for fasting in Jainism are: as a treatment for diseases; for conquest of

> "Jesus Christ fasted for forty days; so did Saint Francis of Assisi. The Tibetan saint Milarepa and the Jain prophet Mahavir fasted more often than they took food. Even Sufi saints like Rabia, Baiyazid, and Junaid, often undertook fasts lasting many days."

hunger; and to overcome attachment to food. However, the period of fasting must be utilized for scriptural study. The tapas of fasting without scriptural study is equal to voluntary starving. Fasting becomes tapas only when the person observing it does not entertain any inauspicious thought, when it does not result in physical weakness, and when the functions of mind, speech and body remain unimpaired. Jain scriptures enjoin that a person should undertake fasting after taking into consideration his physical strength, stamina, faith, state of health, place, and time. Subjugation of senses is also described as fasting and, therefore, those who have conquered their senses are said to be fasting although they may be taking food. The purity attained by one well-versed in scriptures, though regularly taking food, would be many times more than the purity attained by a person ignorant of scriptures, even though he may fast for two, three, four, or five days. During the period of fasting, speaking harsh words, anger, abusing others, or hurting anyone in any way, as well as carelessness, must be avoided. Further, continence must be observed, and time must be spent in scriptural study and meditation on the nature of the Self.

Fasting can be done unto death or for a limited period of time. Fasting for one, two, four, or even eight days, as tapas, is quite popular among Jain monks, and even lay devotees, especially women. Fasting on alternate days and auspicious days for one full year, called *varshitapa*, is regarded very highly and many undertake it. Apart from this, there are various other more rigorous fasts which some ascetics undertake.

(2) Partial Fasting (*avamodarya*). This means taking less food than required to appease hunger. It helps in restraining of senses, control of sleep, meditation, and performance of obligatory duties enjoined by the scriptures.

(3) *Bhikshcharya* or *Vrittiparisamkhyana*. This tapas, too, is concerned with the control of food and is for monks. The ascetic decides beforehand the manner in which he is going to accept alms, the number of houses to be visited, the type of food, the particulars of the person giving alms, etc. He accepts food only when all the conditions are fulfilled, otherwise he goes without food. Sometimes the conditions are too difficult to be fulfilled, and the monk goes without food for many days.

(4) *Rasaparityaga*. This, again, pertains to food, and consists in giving up palatable food in general — milk, curd, ghee, oil, sugar, and salt, in particular. The monk does not live to eat, but eats to live. The purpose of this tapas is to subdue the senses, to overcome sleep, and to achieve unobstructed study of scriptures.

(5) Residence in Lonely Places (*vivikta-sayyasana*). A monk should choose for his residence a secluded place unfrequented by women, worldly-minded people, and animals. This helps in the observance of the vow of chastity and the practice of meditation and introspection.

(6) Mortification of the Body (*kayaklesha*). This consists of the infliction of some pain to the body by adopting certain postures like *virasana*, or by exposing it to extremes of heat and cold. The purpose of this austerity is to develop forbearance and to counteract inordinate attachment to pleasure.

Jain scriptures clearly point out that the practice of these external austerities must not produce mental unrest or hinder in any way the practice of other moral and spiritual disciplines. On the contrary, they must reduce body-consciousness and enhance spiritual insight. They must always lead to internal austerities. Interestingly and insightfully, the knowledge acquired in a convenient situation vanishes when one is exposed to inconvenience. So an aspirant must not hesitate to expose him/herself to inconveniences according to his capacity.

Internal Tapas

(1) Atonement (*prayaschitta*). Acts done for the atonement of sins are called prayascitta, and are given great importance in all religions because they absolve the person of the sense of guilt, purify him, and help him to tread again the path of virtue. Prayaschitta consists in voluntarily confessing all transgressions and gladly accepting the punishment for them so as not to form a habit of repeatedly committing the same mistake. It is considered tapas because it helps in the expiation of evil karmas.

The subject of prayaschitta and its various aspects is dealt with in great detail in Jain scriptures. In fact, there are as many prayaschittas as there are shades of faults or transgressions. Hence it is almost impossible to draw up an exhaustive list of all of them.

While prescribing prayaschitta, the general character and conduct of the transgressor, his capacity to bear the punishment, time, place, whether the sin has been committed once or repeatedly, willfully or by mistake, etc., must be taken into consideration. Some minor faults are atoned just by voluntary confession, while others need serious addressing. Ten prayaschitas in the order of severity have been described in Jain scriptures. These are: confession; repentance; discrimination; renunciation; penance; partial reduction of monastic seniority; absolute exclusion from monkhood for a specific period of time and reordination thereafter; expulsion from the monastic order; and reiteration of faith.

An unintentional or intentionally committed evil act must be confessed with an unperturbed mind, just as a child guilelessly tells his mother about all the good and bad acts done by him. He who expresses all frankly and honestly becomes pure and free from mental agony. It is said that one must not conceal one's defects from a benevolent king, a physician, and a teacher.

(2) Humility (*vinaya*). Humility is considered the foundation of religious life and the basic virtue in Jainism. It is the gate-

way to liberation. Through humility one can acquire self-control, penance, and knowledge. How can there be religion or penance in one who is not humble? By humility one honors the acharya and the sangha. If one elder is insulted, it amounts to insulting all. If one is venerated, all are venerated.

To rise from one's seat on the arrival of an elder, to welcome him with folded hands, to offer him a seat, to serve him with devotion — these constitute humility. There are, according to Jain scriptures, five kinds of humility which encompass all the important aspects of monastic conduct, such as the humble acceptance of the Jain tenets (*darshana-vinaya*), diligent acquisition of knowledge (*jnana-vinaya*), careful conduct (*charitra-vinaya*), practice of tapas (*tapa-vinaya*), and humble behavior (*aupacharika-vinaya*). It is therefore said that one must not abandon humility at any cost. Even a person possessing little knowledge of scriptures can annihilate karma if he is humble.

(3) Service (*vaiyavritya*). Service rendered to the acharya, the *upadhyaya*, an ascetic, an old monk, and other religious people, is considered an important internal austerity in Jainism. It consists in providing the individual with bed, residence, seat, arranging for his food, medicine, reading out scriptural texts to him, etc. It also includes offering protection to monks, taking care of one who is fatigued along the way, or who is threatened by thieves or wild animals, by officials, obstructed by an impassable river, or afflicted by disease or famine.

(4) Scriptural Study (*svadhyaya*). Scriptural study forms a very important part of the life of a monk. It is essential for intellectual excellence. It helps in the development of detachment, offers a healthy engagement for the mind, augments the quality of tapas, and leads to purification from the transgression of vows.

Scriptural study has five parts: (i) reading or listening; (ii) asking questions to dispel doubts; (iii) repetition and revision of what has been read; (iv) contemplating deeply on what has been read; and (v) delivering religious discourses opening with auspicious chants. It must be done with devotion, without desire for praise or honor, and with the sole purpose of expiation of karmas. Scriptural study helps in the control of senses, body, mind, and speech, and increases concentration of mind. Meditation is a crucial means for the destruction of karmas. Meditation, again, is perfected by knowledge, which is obtained by studies. Hence, one must always engage in acquiring knowledge through studies. All of this is why scriptural study is considered the foremost among the twelve austerities.

(5) Bodily Steadiness (*kayotsarga*). A monk who makes no movement while lying, sitting, or standing, and checks all activities of his body is said to be observing the tapas of bodily steadiness. The benefits of the practice of bodily steadiness are: removal of mental and physical lethargy; attainment of equanimity for pleasure and pain; obtaining enough opportunity for deep reflection; and enhancing the power of concentration for meditation. Since bodily steadiness is beneficial in acquiring mental concentration, alertness, and forbearance, it is classed as one of the internal tapas, even though it is concerned with the physical body.

According to another version, renunciation (*vyutsarga*) is the fifth tapas. This is of two types: external renunciation (*dravyavyutsarga*) and internal renunciation (*bhavavyutsarga*). External renunciation includes renouncing attachment to the body, giving up dependence upon the monastic order (*gana-vyutsarga*), living away from the community in solitude for the sake of spiritual practices, and reducing and renouncing the articles of daily use such as clothes, begging bowl, etc. Internal renunciation consists in giving up anger, egoism, attachment, greed, the feeling of aversion or attraction, and unnecessary activities of body, mind, and speech.

(6) Meditation (*dhyana*). Meditation occupies the most important place in the scheme of Jain ethics. In fact, all ethical disciplines are aimed at perfecting meditation. As is stated, *"If a person is free from attachment, hatred, delusion, and activities of mind, speech, and body, he becomes filled with the fire of meditation that burns all auspicious and inauspicious karmas."*

In Jainism, all concentrated thinking is called meditation. However, only two types of auspicious thinking, called *dharma* and *sukla-dhyana*, fall under the category of the sixth internal tapas. For meditation, the meditator should sit in the *palyanka* posture, control all activities of mind, speech, and body, fix the gaze of his eyes on the tip of the nose, and inhale and exhale his breath slowly. Having condemned his evil conduct, given up carelessness, and steadied his mind, he ought to undertake meditation until the thing meditated upon appears as if standing in front of him.

A thorough understanding of the nature of mundane existence, absence of attachment and aversion, fearlessness, desirelessness, and having an attitude of indifference towards the world, are the qualifications for attaining success in meditation. The types and subtypes of the dharma and sukla-dhyana, the detailed techniques, qualifications, etc., are described in great detail in Jain scriptures. Here it has been mentioned only as one of the types of tapas.

This, then, is a short account of tapas in Jainism. Practices like service, humility, scriptural study, renunciation, and meditation, are accepted in all the religions of the world, even though they may or may not be classed as austerities. Controversy arises only with regard to certain methods of physical mortification. According to Vyasa's commentary on the *Yoga Sutras of Patanjali*, tapas essentially means physical mortification. In Christianity, external mortification consists in control of the five senses of knowledge. On the other hand, Buddhism and the Gita do not seem to advocate physical austerities. Nevertheless, the place of judicious external mortification in the scheme of spiritual practice cannot be denied, and in this respect the classification and arrangement of austerities in Jainism are worth appreciating.

Monasticism and Service

Jainism is a religion preeminently oriented toward monasticism. It advocates personal salvation, or *moksa*, as the final goal of human life. The path prescribed is *nivrtti*, or gradual withdrawal from social duties and responsibilities. It is natural, therefore, that in Jainism there would be very little reference to service as it is generally understood. But no religion can spread, become popular, and survive for more than two and a half millennia, without reference to social obligations. Jainism responds to social responsibilities and challenges by teaching nonviolence, dharma, charity, and selfless service.

> "Scriptural study helps in the control of senses, body, mind, and speech, and increases concentration of mind. Meditation is a crucial means for the destruction of karmas. Meditation, again, is perfected by knowledge, which is obtained by studies. Hence, one must always engage in acquiring knowledge through studies."

The five yamas described in the Yoga Sutras — nonviolence, truthfulness, non-stealing, chastity, and non-possessiveness — form the bedrock of Jain ethics. They are the five great vows (*mahavratas*) of a Jain monk and are observed in a less rigorous form (*anuvrata*) by the Jain householder. It must be noted that these values are all socially oriented and are aimed not only at the total emancipation of the person who observes them, but also at the construction of a sane, tension-free society. It is argued that if the five great virtues — especially nonviolence (*ahimsa*) and non-possessiveness (*aparigraha*) — are practiced by all to the best of their ability, there would be very little need left for social service. Conversely, if service is performed disregarding the values mentioned above, it will not lead to lasting good. Thus Jainism lays stress on the purification of the means of service rather than on service itself.

Social Responsibility of Jain Monks

On closer scrutiny it will be observed that social functions have been assigned to the leaders and members of the monastic order, as well as to the lay followers. Even the highest honor accorded to the revered founders, *Tirthankaras*, is due to their role as saviours of society. After spiritual illumination, there remained nothing for them to do. But out of compassion for the world, and with the express desire to help all creatures, these prophets preached the tenets of the faith and showed the path to salvation. The epithets used for them include *lokanatha, lokhitakara* and *lokapradipa*, all of which refer to their functions as well-wishers and saviours of the world.

Although a Jain monk's primary duty is to perform his personal spiritual practices to attain *moksa*, there are certain social obligations which he must fulfill. He is responsible for keeping the moral fabric of the society intact by preaching, and by setting an example through his own conduct. To enhance the glory of the sangha, the monastic community to which he belongs, is his second important social duty. The *acarya* and the *gani* are specially responsible for the protection of the sangha. Monks must see to it that the faith of the devotees does become lukewarm. They must employ all justifiable means to increase the fervor of their followers. A monk must serve his fellow monks, paying special attention to the old and infirm. He must be careful not to cause inconvenience to any of his monastic brothers. An important function of the male monastic member is to protect the nuns from hostile and anti-social elements.

Social Responsibilities of Jain Lay Devotees

The ten dharmas or duties described in the *Thananga Sutra*, one of the canonical texts of Jains, include duty towards the village, town, nation, family, religious congregation, and sect. Each of these social units has certain codes of conduct which a Jain must observe. It is his duty to contribute his share to the various sections of the society. An important responsibility of a Jain householder is to provide food, clothing, medicines, and other basic amenities of life to monks and nuns. It goes without saying that he must maintain and serve his parents, wife, children, and other members of his family.

Dana, or charity, is one of the six essential duties of a Jain and forms one of the four limbs of dharma. Another word used for dana is *samvibhaga*, which is one of the four preparatory vows (*siksa-vrata*) of a householder. The word "samvibhaga" means right distribution, and implies that what one possesses is the common property of all, and others have a legitimate share in it. Giving is the only sharing, and the giver and the receiver stand on the same footing. None is higher, none is lower.

Four types of charities have been recognized: giving food, medicines, scriptural knowledge, and instilling courage. Like a Hindu, a Jain householder must partake of the leftovers of food after offering it to monks. To grant protection to living beings when they are in fear of death is called *abhayadana*, and is considered the crest jewel of charities. According to another list, the four charities are the giving of knowledge (*jnanadana*), fearlessness (*abhayadana*), articles useful for religions observances (*dharmopakarana-dana*), and of goods promoted by compassion (*anukampadana*). Householders can practice all these types of charities, but stringent rules of conduct imposed upon monks prevent them from doing charities involving the giving of food and articles. So the monks limit their services to the spreading of knowledge through preaching, and to making their followers fearless through their teachings and personal example. The householder devotees supply the monks with articles, food, clothing, medicines, etc., so that the monks can engage freely in their religious duties. Moved by compassion, the devotees donate money, clothing, medicines, etc., to the sick, poor, destitute, and to orphans, and also to help animals. The quality of their charity is influenced by, and is graded according to: (1) the giver and his attitude; (2) the way in which charity is made; (3) the articles donated; and (4) the recipient. For example, pure food, free from all impurities, offered to a monk upon the completion of his year-long austerity by a devout Jain with extreme humility and devotion, is an ideal form of charity.

Selfless Service in Jainism

Service is considered one of the six internal austerities in Jainism, and is technically called *Vaiyavrittya*. Etymologically it means relieving suffering through right means. In Jain scriptures, the recipients of service, when and how service is to be performed, and the merits of service, are clearly listed.

> "It is argued that if the five great virtues — especially nonviolence (ahimsa) and non-possessiveness (aparigraha) — are practiced by all to the best of their ability, there would be very little need left for social service. Conversely, if service is performed disregarding the values mentioned above, it will not lead to lasting good. Thus Jainism lays stress on the purification of the means of service rather than on service itself."

The ten recipients of service are: (1) *acarya*, or the head of the religious congregation; (2) *upadhaya*, or the expounder of the scriptures; (3) *sthavira*, or a senior worker; (4) an ascetic; (5) a student or a young monk; (6) a sick monk; (7) the *sangha*, or the religious order; (8) the *kula*, or the section to which one belongs, (9) the *gana*, or a group of three monks; and (10) one's co-religionist or any virtuous person.

The ways in which service can be performed are: (1) by offering pure food and drink; (2) by supplying a plank for sleeping or a seat for sitting; (3) by supplying medicines or applying medicine to the body (like putting eye drops into the eyes); (4) by carefully scrutinizing (*pratilekhana*) the belongings of the monks or the path to be traversed by them so that no insects are injured; (5) by carrying the belongings of monks while they are travelling on foot, or by providing rest to those who are tired while walking; (6) by massaging the feet of monks; (7) by protecting monks if they are harassed by the rulers, thieves, dacoits, or wild animals; (8) by helping monks to cross a river or leave an area affected by famine or epidemic and go to a more congenial place; (9) by removing the excreta of sick, old, and infirm monks; 10 to help them turn on their sides or sit up, when they are weak or infirm, etc.

Service is highly extolled, and is classed as an internal austerity because, although it does not outwardly appear as an austerity, it purifies the mind and greatly helps in expiating past karmas. It helps both the server and the served and cements the bond of monastic brotherhood. It is an expression of one's love for the teachings of the *Jina* and for the sangha (*pravacana-vatsalya*). It is a means for the attaining of faith, devotion, and even samadhi. In merit, service is equivalent to worship, pilgrimage, and austerity. It helps one to reattain the state of faith if one has slipped from it. He who, in spite of being able, does not engage in service, strays away from the path, goes against the teaching of the *Jina*, and may ultimately betray the faith or the sangha.

Service is even higher than *svadhyaya* or study of scriptures, which is another internal austerity. A monk who engages in study alone and does not serve helps only himself, and will have to seek the help of one who does service when in need. A monk adept in service is called *prajna-sramana* because he is endowed with humility, renunciation, and self-control, and is the protector of the whole sangha. However, while doing service a monk must be careful not to injure creatures or do anything which may tarnish his vow of *ahimsa*.

There is not much difference between the concepts of service in the *Svetambara* and the *Digambara* sects of Jainism except that in the Svetambara sect, the householders are not allowed to render personal service to monks; only monks do *vaiyavrittya tapas*. Of course, acts like protecting monks against thieves and wild animals, and taking them across a river etc., can be done only by householders. In the Digambara sect, the lay devotees are allowed to serve the monks personally, and such a service is considered highly meritorious. Apart from this, the service of a lay Jain takes the form of observing the basic ethical tenets, fulfillment of his duties, and performing acts of charity.

Contemporary Service Programs

A number of attempts have been made in recent times to meet the demands of society without compromising the basic Jain principles, especially ahimsa. Jain acaryas and thinkers have realized that there is a greater need for ahimsa today than ever before. A large number of Jain charitable trusts and institutions have sprung up in India, and are carrying on philanthropic activities. The *Terapanthi Jain Sangha* under the leadership of Acharya Tulsi is by far the most progressive, and is a source of inspiration to a large number of Terapanthi institutions in India. The Jain *Swetambar Terapanthi Mahasabha* publishes a periodical and Jain scriptural literature, and runs educational institutions. Another institution at Ranavasa in Rajasthan runs a residential college open to students of all sects. *Adarsha Sahitya Sangha* has published more than 150 books during the last 44 years. The *Terapanthi Youth Wing* has 150 branches all over India through which the youth are trained to live a life of morality and nonviolence. The Youth Wing has as its motto "Cooperation, service and self-culture" (*Sanghatan, Seva, Samskara*), and organizes youth camps, competitions, conferences, blood donation camps, eye-operation camps, camps for treatment of asthma and epilepsy, and conducts relief during natural calamities. Its other activities include distribution of fruits and clothing to orphans and patients, books to needy students, anti-drug campaigns, running libraries, reading rooms, and medicine-banks. The women's wing, *All India Terapanthi Mahila Mandal*, has more than 300 centers in India through which activities for the upliftment of women are carried out. This wing has provided artificial limbs to more than 500 handicapped people. It also organizes eye-camps, blood donation camps, distribution of medicines, etc. It arranges for the adoption of poor children into well-to-do families, and provides for the maintenance and education of such children. Another association gives pecuniary help to poor widows and patients, and scholarships to poor students. Jain devotees also run centers where the sick, old, and infirm Jain monks can be treated and nursed with utmost care and devotion.

Jain Vishva Bharati, established in 1970, is an educational and research institute which has been given the status of a university. It conducts post graduate, diploma, and certificate courses in Jainology, linguistics (especially *Prakrit*), meditation, the art of living, and conducts research in Peace and Nonviolence. The most important section, however, is the one which deals with spiritual practices, where scriptures are taught and training given in meditation, asana, pranayama, and cultivation of awareness. All are welcomed without any sectarian bias. Apart from these spiritual and educational activities, the Jain Vaishva Bharati also conducts a primary school, four Ayurvedic hospitals, and three hundred adult educational centers in villages. Spiritual training is provided by the monks, who are also the chief source of inspiration, guidance, and encouragement for all other activities of the institution.

Conclusion

All told, the ideal of service in Jainism is not much different from what prevailed in ancient Hindu Society. The stress on duty, charity, austerity, and moral values, is similar to what is advocated in the Bhagavad Gita. Even the exemption from service for monks is common to both traditional Hindu monks and Jain monks, though for entirely different reasons. Service is an effective means to Self-realization and, conversely, the struggle for Self-realization by conquering one's selfishness, aversion, and attachment is the best form of service one can render to society.

A former editor of the Vedanta Keshari, and previously of the Ramakrishna Mission Home of Service, Swami Brahmeshananda is a senior monk of the Ramakrishna Order and until recently was the Secretary of the Ramakrishna Mission Ashrama in Chandigarh, India. Over the years his writings in Hindi and English have appeared in several journals, including *Prabuddha Bharata*, *Vedanta Keshari*, and *Nectar of Nondual Truth*. He specializes in themes related to Jainism. He is now retired and is living in Varanasi.

A Testament to the Jain Religion

Namo Arihantanam
I bow to the enlightened souls

Namo Siddhanam
I bow to the liberated souls

Namo Ayariyanam
I bow to religious leaders

Namo Uvajjhayanam
I bow to religious teachers

Namo Loe Savva Sahunam
I bow to all the monks in the world

Eso Panca Namokkaro Savva Pavappanasano

Mangalanam ca Savvesim Padhamam Havai Mangalam

"A living body is not merely an integration of limbs and flesh, but it is the abode of the soul which potentially has perfect perception (Anant-darshana), perfect knowledge (Anant-jnana), perfect power (Anant-virya), and perfect bliss (Anant-sukha). Killing a living being, then, is killing one's own self; showing compassion to a living being is showing compassion to oneself. He who desires his own good should avoid causing any harm to any living being. The being whom you want to kill is the same as you yourself; the being whom you want to keep under obedience is the same as you yourself."

Lord Mahavir (Samana Suttam, 147-159)

◆ Annapurna Sarada

TRUTH & KARMA
The Effect of Pure Speech on the Field of Action

"It is said that truthfulness alone constitutes the spiritual discipline of the Kali yuga. If a man clings tenaciously to truth he ultimately realizes God. Without this regard for truth, one gradually loses everything."
Sri Ramakrishna (Gospel of Sri Ramakrishna, p. 312)

What happens if we do not cling tenaciously to truth? What is the relationship between truthfulness in one's thoughts, words, and deeds and the world we live in? Even to ask this question, will, no doubt, bring to mind for many of us the current plight of individuals, families, communities, nations, the physical environment – our whole planet. Sri Ramakrishna's point (above) that without regard for truth one gradually loses everything, is reminiscent of Sri Krishna's statement in the *Bhagavad Gita*: "*Brooding on the objects of the senses, man develops attachment to them; from attachment comes desire; from desire anger sprouts forth. From anger proceeds delusion; from delusion, confused memory; from confused memory the ruin of reason; due to the ruin of reason he perishes.*" (Gita 2:62-3) "Confused memory," often explained as the loss of the ability to know right from wrong, truth from untruth, etc., exemplifies the plight of those who think, speak, and act solely out of desire for certain ends or objects, or for avoidance of the undesirable. Under the press of false identification with the body and mind as the true Self, and with complete faith in the reality of one's separation from all others, people cannot see things as they truly are, much less describe things as they truly are.

Truth and Karma

In the Sankhya Philosophy, Lord Kapila lists eight great siddhis, or accomplishments. These are distinct from the eight occult powers, and refer instead to contemplation of a traditional religion, indepth study of the wisdom scriptures, acquisition and comprehension of Knowledge from the scriptures, gaining a Guru and compatriots in the dharma, and attaining self-purification leading to Self-Realization. These five just listed are considered the secondary accomplishments and are the means to attain the three primary ones: removal of the Threefold Sorrows, Trividham Duhkham. These three consist of the suffering caused within oneself via mind and body; outside of oneself, caused by nature or other living beings; and from "on high," caused by cosmic forces. The suffering that results from these three are all due to the presence of individual and collective karmas, particularly negative and mixed karmas. Karma, in this usage, refers to the result of past actions that are coming to fruition now. Before attaining the three primary siddhis, one will not have relative inner peace (*sattva*), and without this mental peace, higher states of awareness and eventual illumination are simply not possible. As Sri Sarada Devi stated, "*You need peace, first and foremost.*"

In our lives we see that there are "good" people who set their minds to a goal and everything falls into place easily. Even if they meet with challenges, they pierce through them or adjust their approach with skill, fortitude, and equanimity. On the other hand, there are other "good" people who make a decision and everything gets in their way: they get sick, have an accident, lose their job or spouse, a relative dies, or they consistently get invited to conflicting events, or simply lose their momentum. This is not a matter of good or bad luck. These are karmic occurrences that fall under the three sufferings mentioned earlier. Conventional society will accuse this analysis as a case of blaming the victim, but there is no victim here. We dig these holes ourselves over lifetimes, and we can dig ourselves out of them too, over time. It should also be noted that Vedanta takes the long view: the Soul (*Atman*) is birthless and deathless and ultimately unaffected by all occurrences in *maya*. However, the mind ignorant of its true nature is most definitely affected, and if we want to attain realization of Atman, which transcends *karma*, we must set about purifying this mind. This starts with cultivating *satyam* (truth) and other moral and spiritual practices like those listed in the secondary five siddhis.

There are two issues here: past and current karma (actions) creating obstacles, and lack of verve to pierce through them. Lord Vasishtha states in the *Yoga Vasishtha* that current self-effort is greater than past karma. To a person passively accepting his karma as an ultimate obstacle in life, Swami Vivekananda stated forcefully, "*Blast your karma!*" And so we must, and we do it via absolute fidelity to truth, practiced for a long, long time. Swamiji also affirms, referring to the teachings of Patanjali, "*Practice truthfulness. Twelve years of absolute truthfulness in thought, word, and deed gives a man what he wills.*" (Complete Works of Swami Vivekananda [CW] 6.164)

The practice of satyam, truth or truthfulness, is required of all adherents of religion, and is certainly expected of individuals in any society that values moral and ethical principles. Without trust in the word of others, society breaks down. If the leaders of society do not speak truthfully, if parents, teachers, and the greater or lesser popular idols of society do not practice satyam, culture breaks down. This is so obvious that it hardly needs to be said. Qualities that attend on satyam are: sincerity, integrity, reliability, accountability, straightforwardness, fearlessness, faithfulness to one's word, sensitivity and caution about speaking hurtful truths, reflectiveness concerning the accuracy of one's perceptions, and more. As a culture, do we uphold these qualities and encourage all generations to embody them? There is a story from the life of Sri Ramakrishna during the time he was training his young disciples, almost all of whom were teenagers. Rakhal, who would later become the first president of the Ramakrishna Order, a guileless and pure young man, entered Sri Ramakrishna's room one day. The Master immediately asked him what was wrong, for he saw a shadow over his face. What had he done? After thinking for some time, Rakhal could only remember that he had lied in jest to his friends that day. Sri Ramakrishna told him never to do such a thing again. Swami Saradananda describes Swami Vivekananda as a boy: *"When he reached his youth, that zeal for telling the truth increased a hundredfold. He said, 'I never terrified children by speaking of hobgoblins as I was afraid of uttering a falsehood, and scolded all whom I saw doing it."* (Sri Ramakrishna the Great Master, vol.2 p.834)

From a cosmological and philosophical perspective we will see the power in having fidelity to the Word. The Bengali poet-saint, Ramprasad Sen sings, *"Divine Mother constitutes the letters of all alphabets; in each and every one, Her power resides."* Mahat, the Cosmic Mind personified as Lord Brahma who projects all the worlds, is the first transformation of sattva guna, a Sanskrit term for peace and balance, inferring extreme purity at this stage of universal projection. The origin of the worlds is via sattva. All individual minds are contained in the one Cosmic Mind and are similarly imbued with the power of projection. AUM, the "Word," is the primal vibration out of which all further vibrations evolve — from causal and subtle realms of Intelligence and ideation, to this gross realm of solidified thought that we perceive via mind and senses as a plethora of objects and beings. Therefore, as is our thought, so is our perception. Fidelity to the Word that exists in and through all vibrations, which also implies recognition of and reverence for that divine power of projection, will cause the worlds and our lives at all three levels of being to vibrate with peace and balance. If thought, word, and deed are not unified, distortion results and negative karmas also result, individually and collectively.

In Vedanta philosophy there is the Sanskrit term *"apurva,"* which indicates a subtle mental force arising from pure-minded actions. Swami Chidbhavananda explains apurva in his commentary of the Gita, *"A man's yajna (ritualistic worship or sacrifice) changes into mental force, which alone in reality is apurva. The syllables chanted in a Yajna do not themselves become mantras or mental forces. It is the thought or the feeling that really constitutes the mental force — mantra. The purer the man and his motive, the stronger is the mental force. It is the intensity of the force of mind that becomes apurva."* (Gita commentary p. 234, Sri Ramakrishna Tapovanam)

In SRV Associations, we sometimes make an electromagnet with children to explain how we develop intensity and power in our spiritual life, as well as their opposites. An electromagnet consists of insulated wire wrapped tightly around an iron core. Electricity is sent through the wires and this causes the atoms of the iron core to move in a single direction, resulting in a magnetic field. As long as there is electricity flowing, the atoms move together in the same direction and the magnetic field is present. If the wires are not wrapped around the core tightly, or if they are not wrapped in the same direction, or if there are too few coils of wire, the atoms will not be aligned and directed and the magnet will be weak or powerless to attract metal.

Taking this as an analogy, the iron core is the mind, and the atoms are our thoughts, words, and actions. The coils of wire represent our practice of satyam; the electric current is the prana at vital and psychic levels; and the magnetic field produced is apurva, or mental force. If we do not persistently "wind" satyam around the core of our mind, then the prana (electric current) cannot flow properly; the "iron atoms" of our thoughts, words, and deeds are not aligned and moving in a unified way, and thus there is no useful result. All the power of the Word is dissipated rather than made laser-like. If we speak mindlessly and say we will do something but never follow through, for example, we short-circuit the power inherent in mind and thought to maintain harmony around us — as individuals and as a collective. Our spoken word needs to be taken as a vow, no matter how insignificant the utterance, to engender the power necessary to attain those first three accomplishments, to "blast" our karmas, as Swamiji encourages us. As Swami Aseshananda would say, *"If your ideal is high, then your effort must be tremendous."*

The word, Satyam, is derived from "Sat," which means Absolute Truth as well as absolute Existence. It is the first part of that ineffable description pointing to the nondual nature of Reality: *Sat-Chit-Ananda,* Existence/Truth, Awareness, and Bliss Absolute. What is that truth that can never become untruth? What is that existence that is incontrovertible? Herein is the answer to how simply "telling the truth" as a spiritual discipline evolves into Self-Realization. While embodied, and identified with our apparent individuality, we have to regard all relative truths of different perspectives. As mentioned earlier in this article, if we are sincere and humble we will reflect on our own perspectives with detachment. What motivates our current perspective of what is true or, "how do we see the facts" in any given situation? Relative truth holds sway where individual and collective egos are involved. "My truth" and "your truth" are due to egoic perceptions, or to egos interacting at emotional, intellectual, religious, philosophical, or even spiritual levels.

But Sat designates that singular Truth that is never untrue, regardless of time, place, or circumstances, i.e. it is unaltered with regard to time, space, and causation, the parameters of relative experience. A spiritual aspirant eventually wants out of the confluence of opinions, wants to be free from the ever-changing whirl of matter and mind and be at peace — stable, unmoving, all-containing, and transcending. This is attained via discrimination between the Self and the non-Self, between Spirit and matter, the Seer and the seen. Disidentifying layer by layer from the non-Self, searching out that supreme Intelligence within, and taking one's "stand" in It, delicately and determinedly — then yearning for this Sat alone reaches a crescendo and, *"unto him the God of truth comes."*

Story of Satyavrata

One beautiful story about truth appears in the Devi Bhagavatam to express the greatness of the Goddess of Learning, Saraswati, whose love and generosity extends even to illiterate people who mispronounce Her bijam, Aim. It also details the power of satyam for overcoming all obstacles, including those engendered before birth.

There once was a Brahmin named Deva Datta who had no

children. Because it is incumbent on a Brahmin to pass the Vedic knowledge to an heir, he performed a special sacrifice for attaining a son. During this elaborate and meticulously arranged ritual, presided over by great Munis (sages) serving as priests, the foremost of them dropped the rhythm of the chant momentarily while trying to catch his breath. Angry lest the sacrifice fail as a result, Deva Datta criticized him outright for sounding like an illiterate person. The muni was enraged and cursed him, *"Your son will be illiterate, a hypocrite, and stupid."*

Devadatta was horrified, since the words of a Muni cannot fail to produce their result. Vedic society declared that it is better to have no son at all than to have an illiterate, stupid son, especially a Brahmin's son, because he will be repudiated by one and all. Deva Datta tried with many soothing words to pacify the Muni and make him feel the disastrous and useless life he had ordained for both father and future son that he might take back the curse. Unfortunately, such exclamations by adept persons, once spoken, must manifest. Devadatta fell at the Muni's feet with tears in his eyes. The Muni, whose anger had swiftly lifted, was moved with pity, and said: *"Your son, though at first illiterate, will afterwards be very learned."*

In due time Deva Datta and his beautiful, chaste wife, Rohini, gave birth to a son, whom they called Utathya. At the age of eight he was invested with the sacred thread, signifying the start of his life dedicated to *brahmacharya* and the study of the *Vedas*. But Utathya could not pronounce a single word, much less memorize the verses. He simply sat like a stone. After 12 years the boy still had not learned the basic rites. He and his family now became the object of gossip and slander. Wherever Utathya went, he and his mother and father were ridiculed. A day came when father and mother rebuked him, saying that a lame and blind son would have been better than an illiterate brute. But dispassion occupied the heart of Utathya, so he turned to renunciation and left for the dense forest.

On the banks of the Ganges, in a beautiful place, he constructed a hut and commenced to live on the fruits and roots of the forest with a collected mind. He made a firm vow, *"I will never speak untruth,"* and maintained celibacy. For 14 years Utathya lived without rites, without study, without the sacred mantras, without knowledge of the supreme Deity. Day after day he simply rose in the morning, bathed in the Ganges, gathered food to eat, did nothing good or bad to anyone, and slept peacefully. Yet, he felt his life was cursed without knowledge. He reflected on how he must bear this as the fruit of his actions in a past life. Gradually, he became thoroughly unattached to all things, and being peaceful, passed his time in the forest with great difficulty.

Meanwhile the people in the surrounding area came to regard him as a Muni. Since he never told an untruth, they named him Satyavrata, one who speaks only the truth.

One day, a hunter in the vicinity shot a boar with arrows and wounded it. The bleeding creature dashed into the hermitage of Satyavrata. Upon seeing its distressed condition, and filled with mercy, Satyavrata exclaimed, *"Ai" "Ai"* (go that direction). Impelled by mercy and urgency, he accidentally uttered, though imperfectly, the seed mantra of the Devi. Illiterate as he was, he was completely unaware that this was the Devi's seed mantram. The boar hid amongst the bushes only an instant before the hunter arrived, appearing like a second god of death. Seeing the Muni Satyavrata seated quietly, he confidently appealed to him to disclose the whereabouts of the boar. *"Oh Brahmin, you are famous as Satyavrata; I know that you never tell an untruth. My family is starving and this is my livelihood determined by fate. Tell me quickly where the boar has gone!"*

Satyvrata was now in an ocean of doubt, submerged in a religious quandary, and thought: *"Where speaking out the truth causes injury and the loss of lives, that truth is no truth at all; moreover, even untruth, when tempered with mercy for the welfare of others, is recognized as truth. Truly, whatever leads to the welfare of all beings, that is truth; and everything else is not truth. What shall I do to save the life of the boar, maintain welfare, and speak the truth?"*

At this moment, pleased with Satyavrata for uttering Her bijam, the auspicious Goddess opened the door of all knowledge within him and he instantly became a Seer, a poet like Valmiki. Emerging from the veil of ignorance and limitation, full of Self-knowledge and mercy, he now addressed the hunter: *"That force, which sees as Witness, never speaks; and that force that speaks, never sees. O hunter! Why are you asking me repeatedly, impelled by your own selfish desire?"* Disappointed, the hunter went forth to his home. Satyavrata became known far and wide and was celebrated throughout the three worlds as a speaker of Truth alone.

"When this power of truth will be established with you, then even in dream you will never tell an untruth. You will be true in thought, word, and deed. Whatever you say will be truth. You may say to a man, 'Be blessed,' and that man will be blessed. If a man is diseased, and you say to him, 'be thou cured,' he will be cured."
Swami Vivekananda (CW 1.262-263)

"God is realized by following the path of truth."
Sri Ramakrishna (Gospel, p. 162)

"He who is true, unto him the God of truth comes. Thought, word, and deed should be perfectly true."
Swami Vivekananda (CW 4.10)

Annapurna Sarada is the president of SRV Associations and an assistant teacher for the sangha and its children. She also writes a blog for Advaita-Academy.org. To read more about SRV's children's classes and retreats, visit the newsletter archive on SRV's website: **www.srv.org**

Alexander Hixon ♦

ESSENCE OF ADVAITA VEDANTA

Exploring Gaudapada's Nondual Philosophy

This is one of a series of lectures that Lex Hixon presented in late 1987 and early 1988, in which he explained the basis and deeper teachings found in Gaudapada's famous Karika on the Mandukya Upanisad. Transcriptions of two other talks on this subject will appear in future issues.

What we're doing together this evening is not an intellectual exercise. It's an attempt to open up spiritual channels in all of us which will enable us to understand on a much deeper level than we have in the past. We're all coming here with a sense of needing to make a lot of new steps in spiritual life together, and that's what these talks are about. They're not about re-hashing something that we all know. We all want to go into new ground. The friendship and knowing of each other is going to be an important part of this ongoing Tuesday evening gathering.

We have discussed the teaching of "the two truths" — the Absolute Truth and the relative truth, which has been given expressly by the Vedanta, and by Mahayana Buddhism, but which implicitly exists in all the great traditions, in all the full mystical traditions of humanity. Because it's just the way things are, so it's impossible to conceive of this just being an insight that belongs to people in India, and not to people in Europe, Native America, or any place else.

Paramarthika and Vyvaharika

Relative truth consists of perspective. The nature of relative truth is perspectival — it's a whole vast network of perspectives. There can be false perception. In other words, you could push on your eyeball and see two moons in the sky. That's not a perspective — that's not relative truth, that's misperception. There can be mistakes in the realm of relative truth, but when something is perceived clearly and directly in the realm of relative truth, it's true, and the responsibilities and everything else that it implies are real. Therefore, if we see a truck bearing down on a small child, we're seeing it from a certain perspective, but we must go and take the child out — that's our responsibility — and this is true. Absolute Truth, by it's very nature, is a single panorama. There are no perspectives. That's the very nature of Absoluteness. Therefore, all of religion, even mysticism itself, is part of relative truth. Absolute Truth is what It is; It is the Absolute Ground. It is grounding everything that is happening. It's grounding all the perspectives. All the perspectives come inside, as it were, this embrace of Absolute Truth, but It is not contained in any of the perspectives.

One of the important things that we have discovered and meditated on is that the relative truth is not separate from the Absolute Truth. The Absolute Truth is not higher than the relative truth. This is very important. They're not two things — "this wonderful Absolute Truth which is way out there someplace, and then this messy bunch of perspectives which are down here." That's dualism. And this class is precisely about the nondual approach, the unitive approach. What you really have is the Panorama of Absolute Truth, which Itself admits of billions of perspectives, and that's relative truth. So when you say Absolute Truth and relative truth, you're saying just one thing — well, not "thing," but you're just saying "one." In other words, you're not saying two. The Zen teachers say you can't even say "one," because "one" belongs to perspective. Therefore, you get into the approach that the Absolute Truth is unspeakable. But It is definitely experienceable, and It's definitely understandable, and you can say cogent things about It. You're not just reduced to total paradox, or total muteness in front of It, because all of the great traditions have spoken about It; they've pointed at It, and as I said in a previous class, everything is pointing at It.

So, this is not a class in Indian philosophy. We're grounding our investigation there, but what I want are a vast number of different kinds of people from different walks of life and precisely different perspectives, so that we can verify this Absolute Truth together experientially without relying upon Christianity, or Hinduism, or anything. We must come to rely on the nature of Reality Itself, and the fact that we are that Reality. We are Reality. This wall is also Reality.

Gaudapada analyzes the situation this way. He states, *"There is Absolute Consciousness."* One could use any term, of course, but this is very nice because when you say "Absolute Truth," it might sound kind of abstract. But Absolute Consciousness sounds a little bit closer. It's something that's conscious, or we're conscious of it.

Gaudapada goes on to say: *"And it has three modes."* It has three modes of expression, which he calls the three modes of relative awareness. He talks in terms of Absolute Consciousness and relative awareness. The tradition makes this gesture, or mudra, of perfection (shows hand gesture). I think this could be misleading, but the tradition tries to help symbolize the situation. The three modes of relative awareness are these three fingers — objective, subjective, and pure awareness — and the "fourth," or Absolute Consciousness, is symbolized by this empty circle. This is one gesture, not two different things. It's not "God and the world," or any concept of things that are entirely different from each other.

In a certain sense, forget the analogy, because like many analogies, it's too confining. The very highly sophisticated form of Gaudapada's approach does not deserve to be simplified and made banal in any way. We know how sophisticated mathematics has to be in order to describe even physical events in the universe. So we have to become even more sophisticated to describe the nature of the way Reality Itself is functioning as our true nature. Unless you know higher mathematics, you really can't understand very much of physics.

But I'm convinced — and I'm calling this class as a demonstration of this — that every human being who has human faculties is sophisticated enough to deal with this question of Absolute Consciousness and relative awareness. We're given this ability whether we've had education or not, whether we've studied Indian philosophy or not. Probably the only prerequisite is a certain amount of interest in spiritual life. That seems to be a kind of prerequisite, a kind of ripening process. Everyone here has that, and everyone who comes to the class has it. But I don't think that it's anything different from whatever human being walking up and down the street has. We're not some sort of elite. We just represent the human being which, in a mature state, is reaching out for the Truth. It's very exciting to think that we don't need a blackboard with all sorts of complicated mathematics, or a bunch of complicated Sanskrit terms. The working basis is our own consciousness.

Please keep in mind this analysis of Absolute Consciousness (*Turiya*) and It's three modes of awareness (*jagrat, svapna,* and *sushupti* — waking, dreaming, and deep sleep). The main thing to remember about them is that these three modes are not separate from each other. They're dynamic functions which interact. Therefore, we're agreeing on Reality all the time. For example, the taste of cream cheese is part of my subjective awareness. But if we were discussing it, and I was saying that it was a little bit thin, then it already becomes part of objective awareness — it's interpersonal awareness. We have words for it that are meaningful, so that we're not locked into our own subjective awareness at all. There's no sharp line between objective awareness and subjective awareness. Pure awareness is the kind of root awareness out of which objective and subjective structurings emerge. I emphasized structuring — but they're not "structures." "Structure" sounds like too much of a finished item. It's a structuring of awareness that we're dealing with, like a dynamic fountain. And it's all flowing out of a pure awareness which the sages of the Upanisads call *"the space within the heart."*

Defining Authentic Nonduality

It is very important to notice that some yogis and mystics mistake pure awareness for Absolute Consciousness. In other words, they simplify themselves away from the structures; they go into some high state of meditative concentration where they are experiencing pure awareness, and they think, "This is It!" From that standpoint, then they think, "Well the world must be unreal," because pure awareness has no structures in it. When they open their eyes again and they see the busses going up and down the streets, and they see people suffering, then they think, "Well this must be all unreal. The real thing is pure awareness." This is a very serious error in spiritual life, and it cuts away the whole idea of compassion and responsibility which is more essential to high mysticism than it is to just ordinary life.

So Absolute Consciousness is not another state of consciousness. It is not some sort of blissful state where you don't see anything. Absolute Consciousness is manifesting through the modes of relative awareness. This is Absolute Consciousness right now. But the difference between us and a great sage is, we are identifying It with the structuring. The great sage is not identifying It with structuring, nor with the absence of structuring. This nonidentification is pure Nonduality. It is what Gaudapada meant when he called it "Non-touch Yoga."

I sincerely believe — and I wouldn't have called this meeting together if I didn't believe it — that all of us can have an authentic glimpse of this awakening. It's not just something that great sages can have, maybe every five hundred years. I think that all of us, as human beings, have access, or at least glimpses, of this. Even a single glimpse of this, if it's authentic, can change one's life radically, can give immense strength to one's efforts, can actually transform the world — at least as far as transmission is actual.

So, the sage is the most radical "political" person, because the sage exists to awaken beings into Absolute Consciousness. The sage is not some sort of detached, non-attached, disinterested person, but is keenly interested in the most fundamental kind of revolution, if I could use that analogy. It's just an analogy after all, because awakening as Ultimate Consciousness doesn't change anything in a certain sense. We discussed that last week. In that sense it would be paradoxical to call it a revolution.

Verses of the Karika — Nonorigination

Let's try to study four verses. Gaudapada is discussing the relation of all of this to religion. Obviously, we get a sense that this must have a very close relation to religion somehow, or at least to the mystic traditions inside of religion. But Gaudapada says no! It doesn't have any more relation to religion than anything else does, but it doesn't have any particular relation either. This is why I chose this text, and I think this is very important for modern times. I myself am very involved in religion. The five major religions of the world are my basic perspective. But as we said, the Ultimate Truth is non-perspectival. We want to stress the fact that people can come to this from an interest in science, from an interest in ethics, from an interest in art, or from just an interest in the spiritual path per se, without trying to define it as religion — the path of consciousness, the unitive awareness.

I did learn Sanskrit, and rendered a translation of this text. I received a PhD. at Columbia with my thesis on this text, so I can tell you, this is what's really in it! This is not just my own wild idea of what's in the text. That's very important, because there should be an intellectual lineage going on, and there should be a spiritual lineage as well. I should mention here that Sri Ramakrishna and his wife, Sri Sarada, as well as their main disciple, Swami Vivekananda, who came to America in 1893 — is my spiritual lineage — and my teacher who initiated me into this lineage himself did his early philosophical writing on this very text. What's happening here is a transmission of energy, as well as just a class about understanding. Something that was planted in me by my initiation, and by my studies over twenty

> "Gaudapada goes on to say that all thinkers who speculate about the nature of the universe — whether they believe that it comes from a Divine Nature, or whether it comes from matter, or energy, or whatever term they use — he begs to differ with all of them. He states that the moment you have the idea of something coming into being, something creating something, you have two things. That's precisely what the unitive way doesn't accept."

years is now coming forth in the form of this commentary.

On to the verse, then: We can start by stating that the ordinary view among religious thinkers is that all beings, and all phenomena, have come into being from some primary cause. This supreme cause, or Divine Nature — whatever they may call it, in whatever language — brings to birth these individual beings and phenomena like rays of power.

This view is not acceptable to Gaudapada. So we immediately go into a very radical thing, because as I said before, there can be no separation between Absolute Truth and relative truth. For instance, if two beings go into a room, and one is looking from the far end of the table, and the other is looking from the near end, neither of their visions of the room is separate from the room. The room is not someplace else, like across the street, while the perspective is over here. The space and the perspectives are one and the same, but the perspectives themselves are genuinely different. So the two persons are each seeing very different things, and they might have a hard time agreeing on what they see. That's the nature of perspectives. They can be extremely misleading, and that's how there could be religious and scientific disagreements as well. So, the idea that there's an original cause, a Divine Nature, and out of this come these "rays of power" which form various phenomena and beings, is kind of separating the "space" from the "perspectives," if you can see what I mean.

Waking from Dream, and from Waking

Gaudapada goes on to say that all thinkers who speculate about the nature of the universe — whether they believe that it comes from a Divine Nature, or whether it comes from matter, or energy, or whatever term they use — he begs to differ with all of them. He states that the moment you have the idea of something coming into being, something creating something, you have two things. That's precisely what the unitive way doesn't accept. He explains that people of his school teach this view that nothing comes into being (*ajativada*). Now, this sounds like a strange dialectic. Don't have an adverse reaction to this. As we unfold it, you'll see it's a very generous view, since it maintains all of the religious devotion, and the interpersonal love, and everything in its scope. Don't think that something is being stripped away here. Actually, something is being concentrated, let's say, at the heart of everything, which is going to allow for the richness of experience.

Nothing actually ever comes into being. Gaudapada gives the example of dreaming. He never says something like "that street is a dream," or "this experience is a dream." He says it's like a dream. This is a very important distinction. Think for a moment about dreams; we'll be discussing dreams in future classes. Dreaming is a very essential thing — not in the sense of dream symbols and what they mean, but the whole notion of dreaming, and what it means about awareness and Reality. It's extremely important and central.

But basically, when you go to sleep and you dream of a banquet, and there are bagels and cream cheese and tea, it's very vivid. You feel you are eating the bagels and cream cheese, and you're actually talking to the people. Inside the dream it's extremely real. You may be learning things. It is valuable; everything about it. But when you wake up, you realize, "Well, that banquet never came into being!" It was experienced, but ontologically it never actually came into being. Although it was vivid, it seemed to be a real experience, and it had real value to you — you might have even heard some wonderful teachings in your dream, or whatever — it was all just a dream.

More importantly, though, what Gaudapada is saying is that all of this is also true of the waking state. The sage "wakes up" out of the waking state, just like we wake up out of dream. He or she looks back into the waking state and says, "Oh there are all sorts of valuable things that happened there. We had a banquet, we met at Bagel Nosh, we had a nice talk; but that never actually came into being apart from Absolute Consciousness Itself."

This is what I'd like to have you meditate on. Right now we don't have a chance for a full meditation. But during the week, please meditate on this waking out of the waking state, without any denigration whatsoever towards the waking reality, or of the responsibilities involved there, or of the beauty or the value involved there. There are beauty and value and responsibilities in dream too. There are temptations in dream, for example, which conceivably one should resist. There's a whole world of responsibility in dream, and there's a whole world of responsibility in waking. When one awakes into Absolute Consciousness, none of that responsibility is cancelled out. It's amazing. Has anyone ever really seriously considered this? I've been hearing the teaching for twenty years, but I don't know if I've really seriously considered yet the possibility of waking out of the waking state.

Many times, when people read Indian philosophy, and read this text (Gaudapada's Karika) in particular, it's presented with what seems to be an intellectual naivete, because it's a different style of philosophizing than the Greek style, which is much more elaborate, which I'm sort of even using myself. The Upanishadic truths are presented rather simply and directly, so people think it's a kind of unsophisticated notion that "life is a dream," or whatever. But this is meant to be, and it is instead the most sophisticated view of Reality available to us, and even something that only very advanced modern scientific thinkers are just getting to the edge of, to the hem of the real garment. It got totally evolved and presented in Mahayana Buddhism, in the Advaita Vedanta, and I'm convinced as well, in the Kabbalah — in every sophisticated mystical tradition. And people are getting glimpses of it in whatever walk of life they're in.

In another profound verse, Gaudapada states: *"This Absolute Consciousness is therefore never involved in a process of creation or coming into being."* This is a really remarkable situation if you think about it. We're so conditioned by the ideology of "creation" and "coming into being," that even for a second, to have the taste or the glimpse or the idea that there is a Reality that is never involved in production — when this is contemplated, it has an amazing effect on our own awareness. Most of the religious traditions don't emphasize this very much, because their God or their Divine Nature is always involved in "creating" and doing things, or intervening in history — performing in all sorts of different actions which, from the standpoint of relative truth, are very meaningful.

This truth of nonorigination does not cancel out theology. It does not cancel out history or anything like that. But what we're approaching is what the ancient Greek fathers of the Christian traditions called the apophatic tradition in which you can't "speak" about something. The point is, what Gaudapada suggests is that you can speak about this level if you are very careful not to transgress the truth of nonduality, and if you know the subtle truths of it, and that it can help you and others vastly deepen your own maturity. It can help you vastly increase your entire involvement with relative truth as well, including your religion, your society, and all else.

The "Apophatic Way"

About the apophatic way which I just mentioned, it means one can't "pophise" about it. Western theology didn't have or utilize the apophatic emphasis so strongly. The capstone of what Gaudapada says about this will be my closing remark tonight.

We would think that this special bit of knowledge puts us in a strange position. We're involved in a lot of relative perspectives, and somehow we now know that Reality is not separate from us. It is not in some distant place, but somehow at the center of all this. It is The Reality which never comes into being. Knowing this, we fall into a kind of quandary; what to do? Then Gaudapada gives us this kind of radical teaching: *"What we encounter as the 'creation' is simply Absolute Consciousness appearing through it's own modes."*

Suddenly we don't have any problem with separation at all. We don't have any problem with "veils" at all. This is not a mysticism where there are seventy-thousand veils between you and Reality, and you take them off one by one. There is no veil at all. This is It. Mystics and Zen masters say this as well, and we misunderstand them because we haven't gone through the proper analysis yet. We might think, "This is It! Well, that must mean that this sugar bowl is Absolute Reality." But It's not! It is a sugar bowl. This is a perspective. So if you go around saying, "I'm a mystic. All this is Absolute Reality. This wall is Absolute Reality. I am Absolute Reality!," that is just nonsense. To say that "I am Absolute Reality" is one of the most absurd things you could say. Many so-called mystics have tried to declare that, but they're wrong. The I is perspectival.

Now, if they mean something like, "the absolute awareness…", that's all right. But it's so easy to slip and start identifying Absolute Consciousness with various perspectives, even very high mystical perspectives. If someone says, "God is Absolute Consciousness." The retort would have to be, "No, God is a perspective." And depending on what religious tradition, what language you speak, there are all sorts of perspectives about God. Now undoubtedly, ultimately, what people are calling God is That. But ultimately, what every perspective is, is That. I don't want to sound as if I am anti-religious. I'm very involved in religion. But I want to say that there's a point where religion must be still, and where we have to make this kind of deeper investigation. The moment you assume that you've understood what I've said, then take another breath and say, "No, there's more to understand."

Transitory Objects and the Eternal Subject

Let's talk about objective awareness for a while; subjective awareness is another vast realm. There's a point here where we're all in a kind of objective awareness together, shared not only between us, but between the people in the street and the people on the planet, and everything. All this is an expression of Absolute Consciousness. Therefore, we're not lacking in examples of Absolute Consciousness. We're not just cut from It. We're not ultimately puzzled about It either. That's what some great sages say, *"I don't see why you're so puzzled about all of this. It's the most obvious thing."*

But when you have the glasses on the top of your head and you're looking all around for them, it's not obvious. So I would ask you to take these two interconnected themes home with you tonight — the theme of waking out of the waking state, and the theme of the radical presence — together with the impossibility of separating oneself even an inch from It, and the impossibility of forgetting It. If you could put those two themes together in your meditation and thought, then great progress in all walks of life will be the result.

Remember too, that meditation in this tradition does not necessarily mean to sit down and go into a blissful state, and to hum songs to yourself, and to become emotionally moved. It has to do more with a very realistic kind of illumined thinking, such as we've been trying to do a little bit here tonight. It could be done in short bursts. You don't have to sit down for two hours and try to grind something out. It can be done just like very creative scientific or mathematic thinking can be done, when you're getting on or off a bus, or when you're getting into your bathtub.

Zen says that very few people get enlightened when they're sitting in formal meditation, although that's an essential part of the whole process. They get enlightened when they're raking leaves, when they hear a pebble striking against bamboo, and so forth. So, the taste of a spongy bagel at Bagel Nosh — that might be the thing that reveals it to you. It's being revealed to us over and over again every second, so we don't have to wait and say, "Well, I'm going to wait until I have some very high revelatory peak experience." It's being revealed every second, in the peak experiences, in the depth experiences, in ordinary experiences, in everything.

So we can't really cop out and say, "Well, we don't have enough examples of this; we can't really figure it out, because it only flashes on me once every five years." It's not true. It's once every thought-instant, which I think in Buddhism is one-thirtieth of a second. The Buddhist masters can see thirty distinct events inside of every second.

So please, let's go forward in this way with a great deal of courage and confidence. We have all the data, and we have the enthusiasm for it. Somehow, we have been brought together karmically to sit in this banquet of Gaudapada's Nonduality together. In the next class we will go forward along these very lines. Thank you very much.

Lex Hixon received his Ph.D. in World Religions from Columbia University in 1976. From about 1971 to the late 80's he conducted a weekly radio show in New York City called "In The Spirit," interviewing spiritual teachers from around the world. In the years that followed he entered into deep, serious study and practice of several of the world's religious traditions, eventually becoming a masterful teacher in some of them — including the western chapter of the Jerrahi Order of Istanbul with its several tekkas. Among his books are *Great Swan, Mother of the Universe, Heart of the Koran, Atom from the Sun of Knowledge, Mother of the Buddhas,* and *Living Buddha Zen.* For more information inquire at: **www.lexhixon.org** For ITS Series information inquire at: **www.srv.org**

A Patch of Blue

Like Radha I am looking for my Beloved
Seeing Him everywhere
But never quite catching Him.

Is it madness?
I also looked within
Sifting the molecules of my heart
Hoping to find a trace.

Lost to
Glimpse after glimpse
And no embrace
I have become bewildered.
How can I even say
Who are You, and who I am?

Here I embrace even the madness
As the fragrance of my Beloved
These longing tears
As rapture itself —
In this dissolving beyond words.
Beloved!

Amrita Burdick

Wisdom Facets From the Gem of Truth

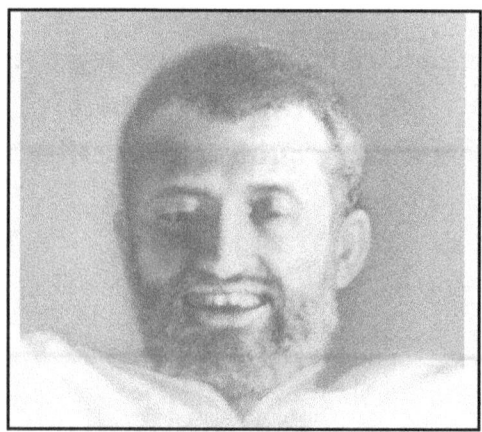

Sri Ramakrishna

Holy Mother, Sri Sarada Devi

Becoming conscious of Consciousness

"Sometimes I find that the universe is saturated with the Consciousness of God, as the earth is soaked with water in the rainy season. Sometimes I see that this Consciousness wriggles about, as it were, even in small fish. Once I saw God in the sexual intercourse between two dogs. The universe is conscious on account of the Consciousness of God."

(Gospel of Sri Ramakrishna)

Admixture of the Cosmic Mind

"In this creation of God there are a variety of things: men, animals, trees, plants. Among the animals some are good, some bad; there are ferocious animals like the tiger. Some trees bear fruit sweet as nectar, and others bear fruit that is poisonous. Likewise, among human beings, there are the good and the wicked, the holy and the unholy. There are some who are devoted to God, and others who are attached to the world."

(Gospel of Sri Ramakrishna)

The Ultimate Prayer to Divine Mother

"Cultivate devotion and love of God and so pass your days. What else can you do? When Krishna went away, Yashoda became mad with grief and visited Radha. Radha was very moved by her sorrow and appeared before her as Adyashakti. She said, 'My child, ask a boon of Me.' Yashoda replied: 'Mother, what else can I ask of You? Bless me that I may serve Krishna alone with my body, mind, and speech; that I may behold His devotees with these eyes; that I may go with these feet to the place where His divine sport is manifested; that I may serve Him and His devotees with these hands; and that I may devote all my senses organs to His service alone."

(Gospel of Sri Ramakrishna)

Please do not Weep....

"My children, please do not weep. You are living gods and goddesses. Who is able to renounce all for His sake?"

(The Compassionate Mother)

"...And Never, Never Matter Changing."

"What does a man become by realizing God? Does he get two horns? No. What happens is, he develops discrimination between the real and the unreal, gets illumination, and goes beyond life and death. God is realized in Spirit, not in matter. How else can one see God?"

(Holy Mother, Sri Sarada Devi)

Mother's Care and Concern

"My children, your body is also my body. I suffer if you do not keep good health. There are certain dangers involved in eating together with others from the same plate, in lying on the same bed with another, and in using somebody else's cloth or towel. Also, a person's good or bad physical condition may be transferred to the body of another. Therefore be careful. In addition, you should know that eating food that has not been offered to God is equivalent to eating sin. The place and manner in which food is prepared and taken is also important. So please remember that pure food brings pure blood; pure blood begets pure mind, and pure mind ushers in the realization of God."

(Sri Sarada Vijnanagita)

Mind Over Body, Spirit Over Matter

"What good are asanas and breathing exercises if the mind becomes concentrated on its own? Asanas and pranayam endow one with occult powers and these lead a man astray. If you practice asana too much then the mind becomes attached to the body. So take exercise to keep the body fit."

(Sri Sarada Devi, The Great Wonder)

Wisdom Facets From the Gem of Truth

Swami Vivekananda   Sri Ramakrishna's Disciples & Devotees

The Great and the Ungrateful
"Those who are atheists, unbelievers, worthless and foppish, how can they call themselves as belonging to His fold? I have met with great sages indeed! It is all very wonderful, and in this atheistic age, they are a towering representation of the marvelous power born of bhakti and yoga. They remain in samadhi but talk to others when they come out. Such sweetness of speech one seldom comes across."

Cry for the Right Reasons
"In India there is a howling cry that we are very poor, but how many charitable organizations are there for the well-being of the poor? How many people really weep for the sorrows and sufferings of the millions of poor in India? Those thousands of Brahmins — what are they doing for the low, downtrodden masses of India? 'Don't touch! Don't touch!' is the only phrase that plays upon their lips. How mean and degraded has our eternal religion become at their hands!"

The High Road
"If you want to give up everything for your own salvation, it is nothing. Do you want to forego even your own salvation for the good of the world? If so, then stem the tide of degeneration at the sacrifice of name and fame, wealth and enjoyment, nay, of every hope for this or other worlds. Then your determination is good, your hopes high, your aim is the noblest in the world."

The Open Road
"He who is alone never comes into conflict with others, never disturbs them, and is never disturbed by them. I long, oh! I long for my rags, my shaven head, my sleep under the trees and my food from begging! That India is the only place where with all its faults, the soul finds its freedom, its God."

(All Selections, *Letters of Vivekananda*)

Dynamics of Parasparadhyasas
"Constant thought of material objects drags the soul down on the plane of gross matter, and produces abnormal mental states and creates disease of the mind and body. It exerts a degenerating influence on the soul. The more we think of material objects, the further we are away from the spiritual abode of perfect health. The continuous thought of body and matter weakens the will-power, and the soul then seeks help from matter and material conditions. This enslaves the soul to the physical body and makes it attached to environmental conditions. Through this delusive power, we mistake the body for the soul, and matter for spirit."

(Swami Abhedananda, *Science of Psychic Phenomena*)

Blessed World-Weariness
"If there is a strong attachment to God and a burning desire to realize Him, all other attractions will drop off. In the life of everyone there comes a time when he feels completely satisfied after prolonged enjoyment of sense objects. At that time, if one comes into contact with a holy man, he feels blessed and prompted to lead a life of spirituality. One becomes dispassionate towards the world by seeing the emptiness of chasing mundane pleasures and clinging to transitory things. Until a man is ready and sees through the appearance of the world, no spiritual instruction will be of any avail." (Swami Saradananda in *Glimpses of a Great Soul*)

Principles are More Important than Personalities
"Are you deep or shallow? Do you live and die in words, or do you live and die in principles? In matters of opinion swim with the current; in matters of principle stand firm as a rock. Be yourself, be strong. Realization is only for those who are strong, pure, and upright. Remember that you are the Atman. Meditate until light flashes into your mind, and the Atman stands self-revealed."

(Swami Turiyananda in *Swami Turiyananda, Life and Teachings*)

SCRIPTURAL SAYINGS
of the World's Religious Traditions

"Things in their fundamental nature are subject neither to transformation or destruction. They are all one single Soul. That is the Soul of all conscious creatures, who constitutes all things in this world – those which are beyond our senses, and those which fall within their range."

"My will in Thee is joy, not sorrow. My will in Thee is faith, not fear. My will in Thee is awareness of my love for Thee. Let my will within Thee be done. For, truly it is life that shines forth in all things! Vast, heavenly, of unthinkable form – it shines forth. It is farther than the far, yet near at hand, set down in the secret place of the heart. Not by sight is it grasped, not even by speech, but by the peace of knowledge, one's nature purified. In that way, by meditating, one does behold That One who is beyond all form."

"And look that nothing remain in thy working mind but a naked intent stretching unto God – not clothed in any special thought of God in Himself or any of His words, but only that He Is. Forsake good thoughts as well as evil thoughts. He asks no help but only thyself. He wills thou do but look upon Him and let Him alone."

"The days of our life are threescore years and ten, and if by reason of strength they be fourscore years, yet is their strength labor and sorrow."

"Gather thyself together into thyself, crouched like an infant in the bosom of its mother. Then look into thy heart and thou shalt see there His image. The soul is veiled by the body; God is veiled by the soul."

"Knowing the Eternal means enlightenment. The holy one attends to the inner, not the outer. All things spring up without a word spoken. Who, by unending discipline of the senses, embraces unity, cannot perish. By controlling the vitality and inducing tenderness, he can become as a little child. There is a being wondrous and complete; before heaven and earth It was. Therefore, the holy one sits with a liberated mind."

Babaji Bob Kindler

Vedanta & Today's Youth

Liberating Human Awareness Through True Religion

"There are two legitimate ways to spend one's honestly earned wealth. The first is supporting the teacher and the dharma. The second is raising one's children in the dharma."   Sri Ramakrishna Paramahamsa

The overall tone and tenor of present day times, even with all its technical improvements, is still only a reproduction of the past. There may come new mechanisms and gadgets, but these only act as accompaniments to real life and, without proper discrimination, called *viveka*, may even prove to be distractions. What is new today will join the ranks of the obsolete tomorrow. To offer a familiar quote from Ecclesiastes, *"What has been will be again, what has been done will be done again; there is nothing new under the sun."*

Further, this ebb and flow of progress and regression is constant, century to century, age to age. Its very movement captivates and confuses the mind, causing forgetfulness of the main purpose of life and its essential components. Distraction away from one's true purpose (*svadharma*) by a host of relative and nonessential minutia, is the unfortunate result of a life lived in repetitive cycles of time amidst a host of changing phenomena. The ancient seers called this and its ensuing confusion by the name of *shatavadana* — thinking of a thousand things at once.

The subject of time in repetitious cycles, *Yugas*, takes on an extended meaning in Vedanta, whose adherents contemplate changing phenomena, but also, and particularly, the Changeless Reality (*Brahman*). The seers of India have seen that, amidst the shifting sands of swiftly changing particles, the singular Light of Consciousness remains the same. This scintillating Awareness, conscious and intelligent, which is our very own nature, oversees all that passes with supreme detachment, and observes its eventual return into form as well, all over endless cycles. As the Bhagavad Gita (*dhyanam*) states, *"We recognize this One Consciousness as the only Witness to the changing phenomena of this universe."*

Bhoga or Yoga?

With regard to relativity, however, the youth of the modern age, in their quite often rebellious stance against the old standards of yesterday, and in their striving to break free of the limitations and experiences of the past lived and laid down by their ancestors, end up merely repeating the fundamental errors of their parents. In the world today, as ruled by the West, that error is called materialism — *Lokayatika Marga*. In India, and for ages, the path leading towards matter, as well as its manipulation and its attempted mastery, was called the *Bhoga Marga*, the Path of Enjoyment. In the higher teachings of Indian sages and seers, the path of *Jnana Marga* is cited as superior, that being the Path of Wisdom. Here, the word "wisdom" does not refer to secular, scientific, intellectual, or technological knowledge only, but more importantly, to the knowledge of Self, or Soul — Atman. Only that superlative Wisdom will bring ultimate fulfillment and, ironically enough, give life in the world its proper orientation. As Swami Vivekananda has stated, *"Spiritual knowledge is the only thing that can destroy our miseries forever; any other knowledge satisfies wants only for a time."*

Astangika Marga — Lord Buddha's Eightfold Path

There is another "marga," or specific path, that falls in between the ancients and the moderns in the scale of time. Comprising the fourth of Four Noble Truths that was espoused by Lord Buddha, it is an insightful look into the problems and solutions of a world society that lived about 550 years prior to Jesus Christ. The Sanskrit word, *samyag*, or *samyak*, pervades its overall tenets. Samyag means "proper," "equal," even "perfect." *Samyagdarshana*, for instance, means equal or perfect vision, referring to the internal or spiritual variety. That vision applies as well, however, to seeing the world for what it is, called *Samyag-dristi*, perfect view. This is the first element of the Eightfold Path (Ashtanga-marga) of the Four Noble Truths, though it matures over time to an advanced stage. There are also: perfect resolve, perfect speech, perfect conduct, perfect livelihood, perfect effort, perfect mindfulness, and perfect concentration. The soul in possession and mastery of these eight tenets is fit for life — both in the world and of the Spirit.

Buddhism and Vedanta, along with Yoga (authentic Eight-limbed, not merely physical), are India's advanced philosophical systems. They are paths of and leading to Truth that are sympathetic to one another. They are shining jewels of India's treasure house of spirituality. They should be thought of as belonging to the same fold, especially considering that Lord Buddha was born in India. The youth of today are beginning to turn towards these salient systems of Truth and inner guidance, but the turn is slow, the numbers, few. One of the great needs in this new, gradual movement, is that western people must become seekers of Truth, going to the feet of masters of spirituality for instructions in seeking It out and realizing It. Secular education, science, psychology, medicine, and the wealth that proceeds from all of these areas are as if useless in discovering and realizing Truth, especially if these modes are taken as ends in themselves (i.e., materialism). As one great Indian seer said, *"You cannot reach the Infinite via the finite."* Forcing the issue with violence and domination-based power is not a solution either, for it fosters so many negative repercussions — called bad karmas.

I The Truth of the Existence of Suffering — Dukha

Chart by Babaji Bob Kindler
Property of SRV Associations

- Sorrow
- Lamentation
- Pain
- Grief
- Despair

(The Five Aggregates)

(Recognition of the Four Noble Truths equals Spiritual Awakening; Nonrecognition equals Ignorance)

II The Truth of the Origin of Suffering — Samudaya
(Due to Craving/Desire)

III The Truth of the Cessation of Suffering — Nirodha
(Due to cessation of Craving/Desire)

IV The 8-fold Path leading to the Cessation of Suffering — Ashtangika-marga

Stage 3 (Prajna) — Wisdom & Insight	**1 Samyag-dristi** — Perfect View	Direct insight into the Dharmakaya; Knowledge of the unity of all existence
	2 Samyak-samkalpa — Perfect Resolve	The stilling of all mental projections; Mature renunciation; Goodwill to all fellow beings; Absence of the desire to do harm
Stage 1 (Shila) — Discipline & Morality	**Samyak-vak** — Perfect Speech	Knowing the limitations of speech; Refraining from lying, gossip, slander, etc.
	Samyak-karmanta — Perfect Conduct	Abstention from profit-oriented work; Conformity with ethics and morality
	Samyak-ajiva — Perfect Livelihood	Avoidance of detrimental occupations; Realization of the eternal nature of dharma
	Samyak-vyayama — Perfect Effort	Freedom from conflicting intentions; Accrual of good karma, avoiding bad karma
Stage 2 (Samadhi) — Concentration & Meditation	**Samyak-smriti** — Perfect Mindfulness	Freedom from vexation/brooding; Sensitivity in regard to body, mind, thought
	Samyak-samadhi — Perfect Concentration	Freedom from opinions; Acquisition of the Four Absorptions of Mind

On the facing page is a chart that outlines the Ashtangika Marga well, based upon the three noble truths that support its foundation. By its components alone, the observer can see how different it would be to be raised in an eastern philosophical system such as Buddhism. Its morality has more to do with the practice and realization of inner perfection than with conforming to human laws in order to avoid sin. Its directives are founded in efforts to acquire higher knowledge rather than in striving to amass wealth, property, and pleasure. Its pristine view is based upon the unity of all Existence rather than on the fallacious belief in supposed divisions between God and mankind, creature and Creator, Nature and Spirit, genders, races, cultures, and religions. Finally, axioms such as stilling the mind rather than exciting it, helping other souls rather than competing with them, and refraining from all forms of violence rather than inflicting them on others, complete the picture. Raising children in this pure atmosphere, *dharma*, results in both spiritual advancement and a truly meaningful life — what to speak of *Nirvana*.

And so, there must emerge from the ranks of the westerner a few realized souls who can act as examples of how, by following paths considered unorthodox and foreign to the uninformed public and the fundamentalist priest class, real spiritual success can be gained. Such examples will go a long ways towards freeing up the thinking process of secularized, scientifically-minded people, seized in the narrow and restricting rut of conventional ways and means. Since older generations are set in their ways, it falls upon the youth to recognize the uniqueness of teachings emanating from living systems of religion and philosophy like Vedanta and Buddhism, and to seek out spiritual masters, even amidst their own countrymen and women, and attain freedom. Speaking to young and old alike, Swami Vivekananda states boldly: *"If you are really my children you will fear nothing, stop at nothing. We must be like lions. We must rouse India and the whole world. Be true unto death. The secret of this is Guru-bhakti. Faith in the Guru unto death. Have you that?"*

Jagadguru, a World Teacher

In his "Garland of a Thousand Questions," the great realized nondualist, Shankaracharya, posed this query: *"What is the one thing to be avoided in spiritual life?"* The answer comes, *"A congregation without a leader."* There are certain individuals whose destiny it is to lead the masses. Shankara was such in his time, around 700 A.D. Swami Vivekananda fits that mold in our day and time. Both of these unique individuals never lived past 40 years of age. In the brief time they were embodied among us, the religious climate of the world and its people changed dramatically, and there was a quickening of evolution in all modes of life and study. When such incomparable beings grace the earth, the pulse of the mental, moral, and physical well-being of the people vibrates at a more salubrious rate.

And it is not just that growth and positive change come as a result of their presence, but, and unbeknownst to many, a host of impurities, like individual and collective karmas, also get purged. This, in fact, and at first, is the real sign that a great soul has come amongst us. Initially, chaos, confusion, and upset may rise up and take the fore. It is as if human beings must come to relish the value of true peace once again before they can reestablish themselves in it. The sensitive soul, the one versed in Witness Consciousness, in equanimity, stands back and sees this fact revealed. Others panic, shy away, or rage along with the onrush of the tides of torturous change. Violence is all too easy to give in to, having become an inbred trait in the ignorant human mind. But nonviolence, *Ahimsa*, is the winsome way of the true warrior. He becomes a Prince of Peace.

Two Vast Wonders — Renunciation & Nonviolence

In all of religious history, at least on the level of collective consciousness, two especially great occurrences have been demonstrated by the hand of God. The first was the spread of Buddhism after Lord Buddha entered Nirvana. Unlike most every other religion throughout time, Buddhism spread across vast reaches of space almost imperceptibly, transforming the minds of kings, queens, sages, savants, warriors, merchants, and workers, effortlessly. Amazingly, this was all accomplished without the least shred or word of violence, and without raising a finger against anyone, any thing, or any country — what to speak of a raising a sword and brandishing armaments. Thus, Buddhism is a "good karma" religion.

The second great marvel, unparalleled in history, current of record and generally unheralded to this very day, is Swami Vivekananda's accomplishment of convincing hundreds of young men to renounce the world and become monks — monks of a new world order whose twofold aim is to gain spiritual liberation after and while serving God in mankind — *"Atmano mokshartham jagad hitaya cha."* A common person finds it hard to give up a few minor pleasures, even when they are harmful to him; an impoverished person cannot even part with a dented and tarnished tin pot; but somehow this great Swami compelled a large cross-section of India's youth to give up the world entirely and take sole refuge in God. This is exceedingly remarkable, by any standard, in any age.

Nonviolence and spiritual growth and inspiration — these, then, are special characteristics of Mother India and Her sons and daughters. On the other hand, being forced by a wealth-seeking government and its violently-based religion to go to war for purposes of domination, or to follow a rebellious political leader into rounds of "justified" violence — these kinds of acts concern power and kingdom. Christ stayed away from them, stating that good people should *"Render unto Caesar the things that are Caesar's, and unto God the things that are God's."*

In other words, there is no personal gain, no glory sought, among those who wage war against the ignorance that causes lust for power and greed of gain in the first place. For, *"What will it avail a man to gain a kingdom but lose his soul?"* Few ever see, nor ever follow, the divinely declared spiritual laws, but hoards rush towards the spectacle of vainglory around romantic ideals, even though these latter always lead to disillusionment and suffering in cycles, again and again. The result? Mankind is turned into man-unkind, and he never comes to know the way of compassionate love leading to peace, in turn leading to the blessings found along the pathway to Self-realization.

A Nonmonastic Ideal for Today's Youth

Few beings, particularly in the West, are desirous of or even suited for monasticism. Those who are, should find consecrated monasteries that are dedicated to God-realization and free from the admixture of politics and business. For all others, a dharmic life is the alternative, one that is based in maintaining a daily spiritual practice involving the timeless tenets of scriptural study, worship, service of God in mankind, and meditation. If dharmic life is attained by householders, illumined souls will get attracted to such families, and children born to such parents will shed light and benefit on every culture in the world. This really represents a relatively short-range fix for the ills of present day life and living, and our young people are key to its implementation.

For immediate results, however, the timely awakening of western youth to spiritual principles and practices is paramount. An attention-consuming obsession with modern technology, as is being seen in these precariously-balanced times, will not promote peace and health, and stands as an obstacle for the most part. For all that they have given, the modern computer and other technological devices have taken over the human mind's ability to go within for answers to personal and collective problems. This dependence on matter fosters weakness of mind.

For instance, *shruti*, hearing the Truth, and *manana*, contemplating that Truth in the mind, have both gone missing in daily life. If one never hears Truth, one can never reflect on It. If one actually looks for and finds bits of Truth, as information, on a computer, and merely jots it all down or repeats it like a parrot, the precious element of meditating upon It within and thereby unwrapping It gets sacrificed. Thus, the joy of knowing, gradual and immediate, becomes lost, and one only lives outwardly, going about the world like an automaton. The overall result is loss of connection to The Reality — the Spirit, the Soul, Atman, Buddha Nature. The eventual result of this lost connection is the onslaught of the four "d's" in precise order — dissatisfaction, then depression, then disorientation, then delusion. Rebirth in ignorance and suffering happens thereafter. One has only to open one's eyes and look around the world for proof of this. Suffering is present among the rich and poor alike; it is just of differing varieties and degrees.

On the other hand, in spiritual life, if it be taught well and followed, the first law of Yoga (Union with God) is, *"All knowledge lies within you."* We have a God-given right, as well as a pressing responsibility, to search within and find all that Is, all that we truly are. It is not a question of whether God exists or not; God is Existence. The guru, or spiritual preceptor, will help the seeker, through well-guided spiritual practice, to develop the inner eye of discriminating wisdom so that he or she can realize this fact of Existence and perceive the infinite wisdom that the soul always possesses, knowingly or unknowingly.

Due Acceptance, Wise Rejection

If we require rational, even scientific proof of this wisdom pathway, then we can try this on for size: The objects of this world that attract us consist of infinitesimal particles of matter that vibrate and change at a billionth of a second. These objects exist in the mind as thought vibrations before they are formed as matter. It is thus the mind that has fashioned them into solid objects, not a "creator" god. Devoid of this essential knowledge, the embodied soul is actually clueless as to his or her true nature, and becomes bound and subject to the six transformations of birth, growth, disease, old age, decay, and death. Unacceptable and untenable assumptions such as creation out of nothing, eternal damnation, nihilism, and the like, are quick to follow the mind's swift descent into this Mayic realm. The Eternal Soul then comes to believe in the appearance of birth and death. But how can something eternal die? Vedanta calls this *"...accepting the unreal to be real."* As Swami Vivekananda puts it, *"The Vedas state, 'I am One, I become many.' Unity is before creation. Diversity is creation."* For most beings, the "many" is the reality,

> "If dharmic life is attained by householders, then illumined souls will get attracted to such families, and children born to such parents will shed light and benefit on every culture in the world. This really represents a relatively short-range fix for the ills of present day life and living, and our young people are key to its implementation."

and the "One" does not even exist. This cart-before-the-horse predicament only leads to suffering in the end.

If psychological and emotional proof of the wisdom pathways are needed, then we can consider the material object from another standpoint — that of a vaunted satisfaction and fulfillment. Empty of substance due to being formed of the "ever-shifting sands" of material particles, all objects have at least five defects to them: they get lost; they break; they decay; they get stolen; or the living being becomes bored with them. Therefore, the belief in God or not aside for the moment, it hardly suits the noble soul to descend to the base level of attachment to and obsession with a world of mere inanimate objects.

On the other hand, again, once the ability to contemplate within is gained via spiritual practices given by the spiritual tradition, all objects, things, relations, situations, and beings, verily transform into outer manifestations of the Spirit. This is where renunciation turns from condemnation to deification. To put this in devotional terms, by loving God first and foremost, the world does not need renouncing, for God takes its place. Authentic Love is realized based upon the destruction of ignorance via following of the wisdom path (*Jnana marga*). There are hardly two better swords to fence with in life than these: wisdom and love (*jnanam* and *bhakti*). Two other swords, called action and inaction (*karma* and *dhyanam*), service and meditation, mature in their wake. Thus comes the wonder of spiritual life.

An Atmosphere for Dharmic Youth

The daily life of a dharmic family would look like this: rising early in the morning for worship followed by recitation and memorization of the scriptures; the essential element of communion with the Ishtam (Chosen Ideal) and meditation on Formless Reality would next ensue. The work of the day could then be taken up, but not without an emphasis on performing all work as worship according to the laws of Karma Yoga. Once a day, as well, teachings from the guru would be imbibed or, failing that due to lack of easy proximity, the parents would instruct the children in wisdom teachings designed to remove ignorance and instill or re-instill natural balance of mind.

This combination of inner practice and outer work ensures equanimity of mind amidst the trials and tribulations of the world, and is thus the proverbial grinding stone upon which the impediments and limitations of mind, intellect, and ego, get worn away. Even the diseases of the body, inevitable in their appearance, will get gradually and systematically reduced, all the while acting as lessons upon which to learn and actually incorporate the art of equanimity of mind (*upekshanam*).

The import of mixing jnana and bhakti has been mentioned already. What is more, the combination of *jnana* and *dhyana* — wisdom and meditation — must be added into this healthy admixture of Yoga, for it will open up avenues to spiritual experience and realization wherein fresh insight will visit the mind in a flood. This deluge will dilute and wash away all traces of ignorance from the mind, and fear and doubt along with it. Lubricated by the warm oil of devotion for God, Truth, Freedom, and all other mainstays of spiritual life, the youthful aspirant will become a fit instrument through which to reach the Goal of human existence, serving God in all beings in the interim.

Spiritual Attainment: What Today's Youth are up Against

As has been already referred to, the presence of the unholy trinity of materialistic science, fundamentalist religion, and a hedonistic and pleasure-loving society, stand as a triple threat to both spiritual awakening and forward progress along the path. To pierce through all these, the panacea of a complete reworking of the human mind on a deep level is to be administered. This will necessarily end up in the hands of what the ancient seers have termed *sadhana*, defined as self-effort, spiritual practice, inner life, dharma, etc. Where this regimen of practice is adhered to, there is found peace of mind and right thinking — as in the Eight-fold Path. Where it is absent, there one sees, in time, the deterioration of society at all its fundamental levels.

To begin on the inward journey, the people of modern times will have to disassociate religion from all of its false associations of the past, and from those purblind individuals and organizations who have dissembled and fostered them. Swami Vivekananda, who brought the West a draught of fresh water and a breath of fresh air in this recent time, spirituality speaking, has put it this way: *"This is a thoroughly materialistic country. The people of this Christian land will recognize religion if only you can cure diseases, work miracles, and open up avenues to money, and understand little of anything else. All these old, foggy forms are mere superstitions. Why struggle to keep them alive? Why give people dirty ditch-water to drink whilst the river of life and truth flows by?"*

To follow the Swami's observances of our culture as given in this quote, and transform these frank but superlative insights into a positive plan, we are first not to allow occult movements and their machinations to masquerade for true Religion. The occult has its own realm, as dreamlike a play as life on earth, and all who are attracted there are welcome to it. But it cannot compete nor compare with true Religion — neither in quality nor in profundity. We must leave miracle-making and mystery-mongering behind and explain the hollowness of them to our youth.

Next, healing is not to be mistaken for matters of the Spirit, since it applies to the physical, mainly, and to the flow of gross and subtle energy and its impedance. However, where healing of the mind, intellect, and ego are concerned, that is the realm of psychology, and in that realm we are to inquire after the traditions of the East for their wisdom methods and conclusions. Why? Because after 2000 years of western culture we have hardly seen any real and true progress in the areas of crucial spiritual subjects. Being bereft in such important areas as internal cosmology (not of outer space, but of inner space), living philosophy (free of argumentation and money-making), conscious reincarnation (which proves that bodies are without number, but the Soul is One), and transcendence of suffering — what to speak of meditation, nondual wisdom, and Samadhi, and the realization of the divine nature of our own innate Awareness — it is far past time for the westerner to beg, borrow, or even plead for higher understanding regarding these crucial principles.

Finally that old poisonous tendency of using religion to open "avenues to money" has to be curtailed. In this world, money can hardly be disallowed, in any undertaking, religion included. What must be avoided, however, is accepting money for teaching spiritual wisdom. Jnanam, as Indian traditions call her, which is unsurpassed for bringing about higher understanding leading to direct spiritual experience, has to be held sacrosanct. It is not to be kept on its ivory throne, it *Is* the ivory throne. Reverence for it as a sentient principle must be engendered in humanity again, especially our youth. As for finance in religion, funds for keeping religion's salutary aims current and in step with human needs can be accomplished via the time-honored way of pious donations from a society that realizes the value of the dharma, or put conversely, realizes that the absence of dharma will eventually result in the advent of confusion leading to chaos — the breakdown of a Godless society. For, as the seers would have it, *"To be good and to do good — that is the whole of religion. Not he that crieth 'Lord, Lord,' but he that doeth the will of the Father."*

Young Aspirants in Vedanta

Vedanta and present day youth are a perfect match for one another, as has been proven by experiments with a small cross section of young people in America over several decades. These yearning souls, tired of conventional religion, and worn down by superficial family life, addicted worldly parents, lackluster educational systems, and the onerous push to gain a profession so as to enjoy wealth and comforts, perk up and take immediate interest when the axioms of the noble Vedanta are presented.

The Four Treasures and Six Jewels of Vedanta Philosophy

"The sages have spoken of four qualifications for spiritual attainment: deep discrimination between the eternal and the noneternal; renunciation of the fruits of action; acquiring the six jewels; and longing for liberation. When these four are present devotion to Reality succeeds. When they are absent it will fail."
— Shankaracharya

1. Cognizing the Distinction between the Real and the Unreal

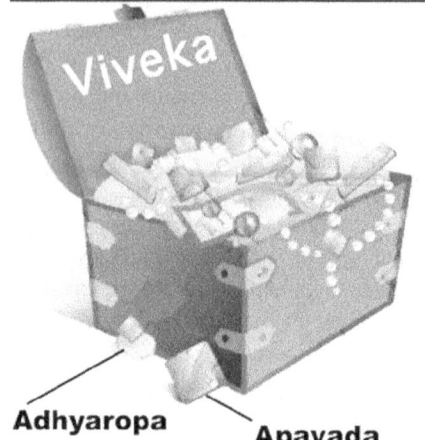

Adhyaropa — Recognizing False Superimposition
Apavada — Refutation of Misconception

"Dejection due to loss, and disappointment at not gaining the objects of one's desire are only stepping stones to Viveka and Vairagya — clear discernment about the unreal nature of the world and the acquisition of indifference to it. Together these conduce to the quiescent state of mind leading to Brahman." Vishvamitra

2. Rejecting the Unreal and Accepting the Real

"Seek not to store up thy treasures on earth, but rather store them up in Heaven." Jesus of Nazareth

3. Locating and Manifesting The Six Jewels

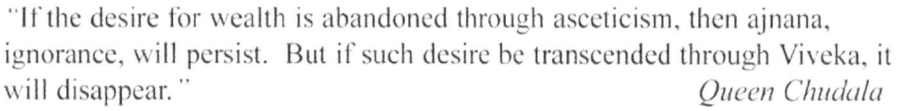

- Sama — Inner Peace
- Dama — Self Control
- Uparati — Self-Settledness
- Titiksha — Forbearance
- Samadhana — Concentration
- Shraddha — Faith

"If the desire for wealth is abandoned through asceticism, then ajnana, ignorance, will persist. But if such desire be transcended through Viveka, it will disappear." — Queen Chudala

"The study of Atma-jnan books, the grace of a guru, ceaseless practice of Vairagyam, and freeing oneself from desires for the world — when all these are attained and meditation on Brahman is engaged in, prana and mind will more readily come under control." — Vasishtha

"Your country is the incomparable state of Moksha. You, Atmic Reality, are the King residing there. Your minister is the cosmic intelligence, and the way to this radiant land is via the pathways of Viveka and Vairagya and the Wisdom that proceeds from them." — Virochana

"Advance towards liberation is the worthiest gain of mankind. May you speedily attain to freedom, and help others attain it!" — Vivekananda

4. Developing a Sincere Yearning for Liberation

Chart by Babaji Bob Kindler

Property of SRV Associations

Vedanta is a double-edged sword that cuts both directions. Its downward arc slices through past karma and mundane life, while its upward swing severs root ignorance to reveal all that was obscured underneath its weighty mass. As the chart opposite shows, it commands one to engage in the process of distinguishing between the essential modes and principles of life and all that impedes one's natural joy and buoyancy (*viveka*). It bestows direct permission upon the soul to extract itself from all involvements that are binding and unhealthy (*vairagya*). It then guides the soul's adamantine search for perfection by providing prime spiritual methods aimed at ferreting out all of the subtle hidden inconsistencies of the mind (*adhyaropa/apavada*).

After the beneficial work of viveka is accomplished, natural detachment settles in. This signals the return of that all-important peace of mind, a quality never to be lost sight of again. The welcome sequence that follows includes the ability to control the senses and their passions (*sama/dama*), abidance in overall balance despite all vicissitudes of life (*uparati/titiksha*), the regaining of the mind's innate aptitude for deep and uninterrupted concentration (*samadhana*), and an adamantine faith in God, Soul, and dharmic life (*shraddha*). Out of these "Six Jewels of Vedanta" rises a sincere desire for liberation — *mumukshutvam*.

Body, emotions, mind — these are immature, "young." Atman, is ancient, timeless. Young aspirants practicing Vedanta will show immediate signs of emerging maturity as the mind remembers its connection to the Atman. Gone will be the weight of ages, cast away the net of worries, and vanquished forever all puerile preoccupations with the empty world of shifting names and changing forms. As Swami Vivekananda promises, *"As soon as human beings perceive the glory of the Vedanta, all abracadabras fall off of themselves. This has been my uniform experience. Whenever mankind attains a higher vision, the lower vision disappears of itself. Madness of love, yet in it no bondage, matter changed into spirit by the force of love — that is the gist of our Vedanta."*

Babaji Bob Kindler is the Spiritual Director of the SRV Associations with centers in Hawaii, Oregon, and California. A teacher of religion and spirituality and a prolific author, his books include *The Avadhut, Twenty-Four Aspects of Mother Kali, Ten Divine Articles of Sri Durga, Sri Sarada Vijnanagita, Swami Vivekananda Vijnanagita, An Extensive Anthology of Sri Ramakrishna's Stories, A Quintessential Yoga Vasishtha,* and *Reclaiming Kundalini Yoga.* Founder and Artistic Director of Jai Ma Music, he is also an accomplished musician and composer who has produced over twenty-five albums of instrumental and devotional music to date.

Spiritual Transmission to a Qualified Youth
Lord Vasishtha and the young Sri Ram

Vasishtha: *"One needs a mind that has dissolved, but which spontaneously retains its natural spiritual element."*

Ram: *'Dissolved mind? What is that? What would be the thoughts and actions of a mind that is not there?"*

Vasishtha: *"First of all, desires, called vasanas, have let go their hold on such a mind. Illusions have also vanished, leaving it clarified of content. Negativities run off of it like water from the waxy surface of a lotus leaf. Anger gets angry at its own abrasive presence and destroys itself in such a mind. Passions contrary to dharma are dispelled, and bright qualities then attend upon it. Though transparent, it continues to operate the five senses, which function free and clear of the selfish ego-mind mechanism."*

Ram: *"From what you have said, there seems to be two types of mind: the original and the ordinary. What are the characteristics of the ordinary mind?"*

Vasishtha: *"That mind is called the crystallized mind by the seers. It dotes on desires and fashions illusions without regard for any suffering that ensues. It thrives on dualities, and so suffers pain and pleasure in cycles. Anger in it acts like a spark to ignite the fuse of passion at the slightest incentive. When deterred, it abandons forbearance and easily gives way to frustration instead. When in a slothful mood, it falls victim to dominance, so lower powers use such a mind for unhealthy and disruptive purposes. Enlightened beings shun it, O Ram."*

Ram: *"This teaching of the dissolved and crystallized mind, dear guru, it is a precious gem. I will use it to cross the ocean of samsara and find peace."*

Excerpt from *A Quintessential Yoga Vasishtha*

◆ Rev. Canon Charles P Gibbs

BLESSED ARE THE PEACEBUILDERS
Some Dynamics along the Path to Universal Peace

*They will not hurt or destroy on all my holy mountain;
for the earth will be full of the knowledge of the Lord as the waters cover the sea. (Isaiah 11:9)*

Over 2,700 years ago, the Hebrew prophet Isaiah offered this stirring vision of universal peace. And for nearly three millennia, from that day to this, the Earth has been drenched with blood as humans killed each other – combatants and innocent women, children, and men – in ever-larger numbers with ever-increasing efficiency and often in the name of religion. Does this mean we should discard Isaiah's vision? Are we doomed to continue this deadly escalation until this sacred Earth is a wasteland of walled cities, an armed camp whose rivers run red with blood? I don't believe so. But to avoid that path we as a species need to grow in the direction Isaiah's prophesy points — toward oneness with the One, heeding the call in the world's great wisdom traditions to be peacebuilders.

The decision to commit to this call needs to begin individually within each of us. It is, as I believe, a call to inner transformation. This transformation is based on an understanding of human nature I have heard as a teaching of the great Buddhist monk, Thich Nhat Hahn, and that I believe most, if not all, of our wisdom traditions express in their unique way. To paraphrase: Each of us has within our self the potential for everything a human being is capable of — the capacity for love and for hate, for compassion and for cruelty, for generosity and for selfishness, for peace and for violence, for gratitude and for self-centeredness, for good and for bad, for openness and for intolerance, for truthfulness and for falsehood, for serenity and for anger, for joy and for sorrow.

Which of these capacities will bear fruit within us and through our actions depends on which of them are nurtured. No matter how we self-identify in terms of religion, spirituality, or ethical tradition, we have a primary responsibility to nourish within ourselves the capacities — such as love, compassion, mercy, generosity, gratitude, openness — that help us to become true human beings, to become peacebuilders; and to help nourish these capacities within others. For Buddhists, this is the path of awakening. For Muslims, it is the greater jihad — the jihad al-nafs. For Hindus, it is following the path of yoga — bhakti, karma, jnana, raja — to our deepest self-realization. For Christians, it is living into Jesus' simple and endlessly complex command that we love God with the fullness of our being, and love our neighbor as we love our self.

Perhaps the most widely accepted expression of this mandate to nurture the capacities for peace within ourselves and others is the Golden Rule, differently but consistently expressed in all the world's wisdom traditions. As a Christian, I grew up with the version of the Golden Rule spoken by Jesus: *"Do to others as you would have them do to you."* I believe the flowering of efforts in the international interfaith movement to promote the Golden Rule, of which my dear friend, Ambassador Mussie Hailu from Addis Ababa, is a visionary leader, is a tremendously hopeful sign that deserves to flourish around the world.

At the same time, I feel compelled to offer a cautionary note given to me some years ago by a young Muslim woman. After a talk in which I'd mentioned the Golden Rule, she approached me and said words to this effect: I mean no disrespect, but I don't want you, an older white Christian male from the United States, to assume that I, a younger Muslim woman from the Middle East, would automatically want the same things that you want, or would want to be treated the way you want to be treated. Your perspective is part of the foundation of colonialism. Instead, I would like to rephrase the Golden Rule this way: Treat others as they would like to be treated.

In other words, don't assume you know how someone else would like to be treated just because you would like to be treated in a certain way. Take the time to ask questions and listen to the answers. That is the beginning of the path to the sort of mutually respectful relationship that is the foundation of peacebuilding. With this cautionary note, I urge any who wish to follow the peacebuilder's path to root yourself in the riches of your unique tradition that will help you manifest the Golden Rule by nurturing those qualities and values in yourself and others that lead toward peace. Many, if not all traditions, offer disciplines of study, prayer/meditation/contemplation, and service, as elements of this path. Whatever your tradition, give yourselves wholeheartedly to these disciplines with the support of wise guides, and you will daily strengthen your capacity as a peacebuilder.

An inevitable consequence of following such a path is that you begin to gain an experience and understanding of the interconnectedness of all life, both in the human community and in the whole Earth community. This experience and understanding lead to an emerging consciousness of the fundamental oneness of all that is, a consciousness that also allows you to honor diverse expressions of that oneness. This allows you, in the words of another dear friend from Addis Ababa, Dr. Semir Yusuf, to be different and one at the same time. Or, in the words of a wise man from Pakistan who happened to be driving the cab I rode in one early morning in New York City, we can cherish both our unique identity — in his case, Muslim and Pakistani — and our shared identity — children of one Source and citizens of the

> "Even if the present state of division and violence makes the prospect of universal peace seem an impossibility, we must dare to imagine the possibility of universal peace and commit ourselves to making that vision a reality."

Earth. This powerful consciousness of unity and diversity is a critical asset on the journey of peacebuilding.

As I've noted above, at the same time we're working on our self, we are doing our best to help others, who we come to see not as "other" but as kindred travelers on the journey toward universal peace. Inevitably, this helps us move beyond being individuals working only on our self to diverse communities that ultimately may find common cause as a movement of people, united in their diversity, seeking to influence the entire human community to move in the direction of peace. While these individuals and communities may flourish in the grassroots, they must inevitably begin to sway the treetops where policy decisions are made that affect the lives of millions and billions of people. The United Religions Initiative (<http://www.uri.org>www.uri.org), which I served for seventeen years as founding executive director, is an enduring, daily example of this evolution.

On this journey, whose blessings and victories will inevitably be intermixed with challenges and setbacks, it is important to hold a strong vision of the desired destination and a fierce determination to remain true to the journey. In his book, *The Moral Imagination: The Art and Soul of Building Peace*, a dear friend and colleague, Dr. John Paul Lederach, offers powerful guidance in this effort by urging those on the journey of peacebuilding to cultivate their "moral imagination," which he describes as the capacity, while rooted in present realities, to be able to envision and bring into existence a desired future of peace. Even if the present state of division and violence makes the prospect of universal peace seem an impossibility, we must dare to imagine the possibility of universal peace and commit ourselves to making that vision a reality.

Dr. Lederach proposes four disciplines as essential to cultivating the moral imagination:

"The kind of imagination to which I refer is mobilized when four disciplines and capacities are held together and practiced by those who find their way to rise above violence. Stated simply, the moral imagination requires the capacity to imagine ourselves in a web of relationships that includes our enemies; the ability to sustain a paradoxical curiosity that embraces complexity without reliance on dualistic polarity; the fundamental belief in and pursuit of the creative act; and the acceptance of the inherent risk of stepping into the mystery of the unknown that lies beyond the far too familiar landscape of violence."

Or, expressed more poetically:

Reach out to those you fear.
Touch the heart of complexity.
Imagine beyond what is seen.
Risk vulnerability one step at a time.

Along the way in this journey it becomes clear that peace is far, far more than the absence of violence, which is why I avoid the use of the term "nonviolence" in favor of "peacebuilding." The journey toward peace not only requires a journey inward to identify and cultivate those qualities and values that lead toward peace and to clear away those obstacles that stand in the way of peace, but also a journey outward to seek allies on this journey to create new possibilities for peace and to confront the obstacles that stand in the way. Part of this effort may be to take advantage of the proliferation of educational opportunities that provide a rich background and sets of skills to help people develop their capacities as peacebuilders. After millennia of investing vast human, material, and financial resources in perfecting the human capacity for violence, at the beginning of the 21st Century we are seeing a slow but significant investment in developing the human capacity to be peaceful.

The journey toward universal peace leads us ineluctably to the issues of basic human freedom and dignity, and of respect for difference. It forces us to confront poverty, oppression, exploitation, inequality, consumerism and militarization. And, consistent with an ever stronger apprehension of the basic oneness of all life in a living universe, this journey demands that we look unflinchingly at environmental degradation, not only from the perspective of its toll on members of the human community, but also for what it is doing to this sacred Earth and our sisters and brothers of all the other species which call this Earth their home. It asks that we do this on a personal level, on a community level, and ultimately on the level of the systems and policies that shape and govern the world we live in.

The United Nations' Millennium Development Goals are the best effort I know of to shift high-level policy in the direction of investing less in militarism and more in the direction of addressing challenges that stand between us and a more peaceful world:

1. Eradicate extreme poverty and hunger
2. Achieve universal primary education
3. Promote gender equality and empower women
4. Reduce child mortality
5. Improve maternal health
6. Combat HIV/AIDS, Malaria and other diseases
7. Ensure environmental sustainability
8. Global partnership for development

While it is essential to hold the full picture of the whole of the opportunity and challenge that faces us on the path to universal peace, it is equally important to acknowledge that no one can do everything. So, building on a foundation of inner work that helps predispose us to peacebuilding and helps clarify our unique calling in this work, each of us needs to discern the area(s) of action we find particularly engaging and commit to pursuing that effort wholeheartedly.

Looking at the magnitude of the challenges (and opportunities) facing the human community, it is easy to feel overwhelmed, but it is essential that we do not. We need to believe in the depth of our being that we are not alone on this journey and that what we do will make a positive difference. And we need to trust that there are forces far greater than ourselves at work to move the human community toward peace.

Is universal peace possible? I believe the answer is yes. Isaiah had a vision of universal peace. So have countless others of all traditions over the millennia. Is universal peace probable? I believe we hold the answer to this question in our hands, and believe that we are held in much bigger hands — which I believe is what Jesus meant when he said, *"Blessed are the peacebuilders, for they will be called children of God."*

Whatever your tradition and whatever you believe or don't believe about God, the Source, known by so many names and in so many languages, and by no name and in silence, in fullness and emptiness, in presence and in absence, in light and in darkness, I look forward to encountering you as a fellow peacebuilder on the journey toward the promised land of universal peace.

A lover of the Mystery, Charles Gibbs has sought to be of service all his life. From 1996 until his retirement in 2013, he served as the founding Executive Director of the United Religions Initiative (www.uri.org), a global grassroots community promoting interfaith cooperation for peace, justice and healing in 78 countries. An Episcopal priest, a visionary and a poet, Charles is blessed by his friends and colleagues of diverse faiths with whom he shares a commitment to serve the world through spiritual transformation and cooperative engagement for the good of all life on this sacred Earth. As son, brother, husband, father, father-in-law and grandfather, he cherishes and is inspired by his family. Mindful of the abundant blessings that come even through life's biggest challenges, he seeks to live each moment in gratitude.

Mark 10:15
"Truly I tell you, anyone who will not receive the kingdom of God like a little child will never enter it."

Matthew 19:14
Jesus said, "Let the little children come to me, and do not hinder them, for the kingdom of heaven belongs to such as these."

Matthew 18:3
And he said: "Truly I tell you, unless you change and become like little children, you will never enter the kingdom of heaven."

1 Corinthians 14:20
"Brothers and sisters, stop thinking like children. In regard to evil be infants, but in your thinking be adults."

Luke 18:17
"Truly I tell you, anyone who will not receive the kingdom of God like a little child will never enter it."

Dr. Nahid Angha

SACRED SUFI POETRY
An Expression of Divine Love

In the history of Sufism we read about a group of people who lived at the time of the Prophet, fourteen centuries ago, and were enraptured by Divine love based on the teachings of the Prophet. They used to sit on the platform of his mosque in Medina, waiting for him to come and teach them the meaning of inspiration, Divine love, and the way towards unity. In search of the inner path they devoted themselves to meditation, purification, and service. It is from this group, *Ahle Suffa*, "the people of the platform," that Sufism derives its origin. Their devotion contributed to the establishment of one of the most celebrated human movements in the history of civilization.

Sufism was developed as the result of the devotion of those few individuals, and over centuries, Sufis and their students traveled across many lands and introduced Sufism into different cultures and times. Throughout the world of Sufism, love remained as the eternal theme. Sufis have gracefully glorified this theme in their poetry, in their principles, and in their songs:

> *Let love exist*
> *No fear if I exist or not*
> *Let this Iron transform into gold*
> *Rising from the fire of love.*
> (Shah Maghsoud, 20th century Persian Sufi)

Sufi poets bring an extraordinary contribution to both the world of religion and the world of literature. Even though these worlds may seem very different — the one, universal, the other, highly personal — yet in their poetic expressions and songs Sufi poets bring these two worlds together in the unity of Divine love. The beauty of their words and the system of mutually referential symbols that form their imagery create a language of understanding that both expresses and explains the principle of Sufism, a state of Divine rapture and ecstasy, into the heart of their listeners.

They speak of the beauty of annihilation of one's self into the Will of Being; they write of the transience of the world of possibilities; of the grace of nature; of the longing of the lover; of the dignity of the human heart. Their words speak to us as messengers of the soul embracing all life. They speak to us through their humanity to our humanity in its deepest meaning. The message of Sufism is always hidden behind the surface of their words in the special system of symbolism that generations of Sufi poets have developed to express their understanding in their sonnets and masnavi, quatrains, and prayers. They tell us that a universe of love demands glory and richness, and their highly sophisticated language of poetry claims an unsurpassed place among the world's poets in creating such glorification of love.

While their metaphors paint the colors of the flower fields, and their rhythms and rhymes create the melodies of the nightingales and songs of nature onto the pages of a book, yet there exists a deep meaning behind each word and rhythm to be sought and found.

> *Neither cold nor hot this fine breeze blows*
> *The dust cloud from the rose garden of desire.*
> *Nightingale singing "Drink! Drink your Wine!"*
> *To the loving heart of the yellow rose.*
> (Omar Khayyam, 11th century Persian Sufi)

Sufi poets are masters of sonnets and quatrains, structures of verse that, in their meter and complex patterns of rhythm, cannot be directly translated into other languages. We are to be mindful that in translations, even though the translator may remain as close as possible to the original meaning of the poet as it is expressed through the rich system of symbolism of Sufi metaphor, that nonetheless, translating such deep principles expressed in a highly sophisticated language into another language that does not necessarily hold the same history, spirituality, symbolism, or cultural heritage, remains difficult — if not an impossible task.

The Sufis express unity in their rapturous state of love, and melt away into the being of the Beloved where there remains no separation, nothing of the lover: all that remains is the Beloved, for there is nothing other than the Beloved.

> *I wonder at this You and I,*
> *You are all there is*
> *And I am all annihilated, no longer exist.*
> Mansur al-Halaj (10th century Persian Sufi)

> *We searched awhile for the Divine*
> *Within the depth of our illusions*
> *Looking there to find His signs*
> *In the beings of "You" and "I."*
> *When love appeared*
> *"You" and "I" were dissolved*
> *And no more need to follow signs.*
> (Shah Maghsoud)

The themes of love and the Divine form the foundation for great poetry, and it is here that humanity is brought into confrontation with the essential. Sufi poets speak this universal language of love, a language that binds every particle of the universe together. They speak of the heart's longing, dreaming, and hoping to find its way to the doorstep of the Beloved. That's all! Nothing else matters!

The rose's song rang out amidst the garden:
Leaves of fine gold, one upon another;
Smiling laughter, too,
I brought into this world of colors.
Then from all this,
My blossom bursting, scattered
I gave my petals to this world
Where nothing matters.
(Omar Khayyam)

To a Sufi, it is that Divine love that leads the wayfarer towards unity. It is the nature of love that unites a lover with that which is loved. In this journey, essential unity remains, and the veils of multiplicity fall, as Sufi falls in love with this magnificent Beloved. The principle of harmony requires a deep and balanced agreement between the longing heart of the wayfarer and the answer s/he receives, there is connection and harmony between the loving heart and the Beloved, between the seeker and that which is Sought.

Sufi Poetry follows the same principle of unity as in all Sufism. Poetry expresses the traveler's journey from the world of multiplicity and dissolution into unity. Through the most beautiful use of metaphors and rhythms, Sufi poets take their listeners to the world of nature and let them see her beauty through the eyes of love and appreciation, where everything manifests the essence of love, where every manifestation turns into a love affair: nightingale sings for the yellow rose, morning dew awaits for the sunrise, breeze of dawn is saturated by the fragrance of the beloved hair, and young lovers are embracing by the pomegranate tree. Through such mesmerizing language they tell us that the Essence of the Divine is hidden behind the changing veils of nature, concealing the essence of Being within itself. We must come to the world of nature and see the core and spirit of love hidden behind such beauty. They advise us not to fall into limitation and let the world of transience takes us away from our humanity, our peace, and our being:

Oh, my friend:
If you have chosen an inner path,
remember that we all are travelers,
our moments are passing
and we are passing with them.
Your wealth will not remain forever
and your pain will not last,
so do not become a slave to your wealth
nor to your pain.

If you are a person of an inner path,
then you are a person of peace,
so make peace with yourself
and make peace with your surroundings.
(Ezzeddin Nasafi, 13th century Persian Sufi)

Sufi poets paint the most vivid colors of the flower fields and nightingales onto the pages of one's mind; their rhythms and rhymes compose the melodies of nature audible to one's heart. Our hearts identify with the longing of the Sufi poet. After all, is there anyone who has not experienced the bitter-sweet taste of love?

Listen to the singing of the reed
To melodies of plaintive separation.
A listener I need
One with a longing heart
To whom I shall sing my songs.
(Rumi, 13th century Persian Sufi)

Sufi poets use many symbols to speak of the Eternal Unity. Metaphors such as "Wine," "Cup," "Wine Bearer," "Drunkard," or "Drunken," "ruins," "annihilation," or "tulip" are most often used in Sufi poetry or prayers to express Divine love and the state of unification. In Sufi prayers and poetry, "Cup," (*jaam*) refers to the heart that holds the Divine Wine; while "Wine" (*sharab*) serves as a unifying symbol for love (*Ishq*). These words express the extremity of Divine love, a longing for unification where the lover is saturated by love for the Beloved. From the apparently paradoxical idea of wine, a symbol is created: for the Sufi does not drink wine, as wine drinking is forbidden in Islam. The paradox is, characteristically, resolved on a higher level by a reference to the Qur'an: "... *And their Lord will give them a drink of Wine, Pure and Holy.*" (76:21, Al-Insan)

Thus, the Sufi poet uses the metaphor of wine to refer to *sharaban tahura*, the pure wine. In all Sufi poetry and prayers, the Sufi becomes drunk from this pure wine. The Divine, the eternal Beloved of all, is expressed by the figure of the wine bearer, who offers this wine and pours it into the cup (the heart) of those who are fit to receive it:

A vessel of Wine, a book of Love
A loaf of bread to pass the time,
And You and I are in the ruins,
A feast beyond the dream of a king
(Omar Khayyam)

Sun has thrown the cover of morning upon the roof
King has poured the Wine into the Cup
"Drink!" the Caller at Dawn announced: "Drink!"
A melody echoed in the cycles of time.
(Omar Khayyam)

On the journey of the heart, we each walk alone, and worship the Divine in the solitude and privacy of our hearts. The great world of ecstasy is hidden within the nature of humankind. Each human becomes a galaxy, and each galaxy lives in harmony with the universe, within and without.

In Sufi Poetry, words are woven together by these masters with exceptional experiences of love; in each verse they bring unique feelings into the heart of their listeners. Yet ultimately what they teach us, as all Sufis do, is to walk the path towards the Divine and look within to discover the treasure of Being, a treasure beyond all measures:

> When I was young my soul's sphere searching for
> Your Tablet and Pen, Heaven and Hell;
> The Master called, the secret told:
> you are the tablet and pen, heaven and hell, and all.
> (Omar Khayyam)

Quotations and excerpts are from:
Ecstasy: The World of Sufi Poetry and Prayers, by Nahid Angha, (Calif: IAS Publications, 2nd Edition, 2007).

Nahid Angha, Ph. D., a Co-Director of the International Association of Sufism (IAS), the Executive Editor of the quarterly journal, *Sufism: An Inquiry*, and founder of the International Sufi Women Organization. Dr. Angha has created an intra-faith movement within Sufism through annual Sufism Symposium hosting Sufi masters from the globe for a weekend dialogue. She is the main representative of the IAS to the United Nations (NGO/DPI), a human rights advocate, an inductee to the Marin Women's Hall of Fame. An internationally published author, she is one of the major Muslim Sufi scholars and leaders of the present time with over fourteen published books, has given lectures and taught classes for over thirty years, including speaking engagement at the United Nations; Smithsonian Institute; His Majesty Mohammed IV's First International Conference on Sufism, Morocco; Women in Islam, S. Africa; Science and Spirituality, Italy, and more.

Dive Deep, O Mind

Dive deep, O mind, dive deep in the Ocean of God's Beauty.

If you descend to the uttermost depths, there you will find the gem of Love.

Go seek, O mind, go seek Vrindavan in your heart, where with His loving devotees Sri Krishna sports eternally.

Light up, O mind, light up true wisdom's shining lamp, and let it burn with steady flame unceasingly within your Heart.

Who is it that steers your boat across the solid earth? It is your guru, says Kubir. Meditate on his Holy Feet.

Kubir

◆ Shivakumar Viswanathan

NONCOMPROMISE IN ADVAITA VEDANTA
Advaita: A Philosophy and a Solution

The problem of root ignorance is one that is taken on by every deep and profound seer and philosopher who takes embodiment on earth. But it is not the only main problem to be dealt with. The Truth that these superlative beings bring with them out of formless samadhi is subject to misinterpretation by small and narrow minds, which weakens its potency and lessens its effectivity in curing the disease of ignorance. It is therefore that illumined souls point out the mistake of compromise to sincere souls seeking the highest ideal.

Is Advaita Vedanta a mere archaic philosophy that ancient Indians came up with? Nothing could be farther from the truth. In fact, Advaita is more than mere philosophy and is actually a solution to a problem. As we see in Mathematics, when a particular problem is to be solved, a specific approach is taken to arrive at a final solution. Misuse the formula and the results go awry. Advaita Vedanta is pretty much like that. It is an approach to the problem of samsara. Advaita is the perfect solution to the quagmire of limitation and bondage, of delusion and suffering.

Scientists use experiments and set up the condition, parameters, and the environment very carefully for the experiment to succeed. In fact, they study many things that have been touched upon by the scriptures. For example, modern day psychologists analyze dreams. However, their intention is completely different from the scriptural analysis of dreams and the other states of our experience. The scientist will analyze and come up with a clean interpretation of dreams and explain why an individual has certain complexes in his life. The scriptures, on the other hand, analyze the three states of waking, dream, and deep sleep to arrive at their ontological status. So any uncompromising stand that one sees in Vedanta is not due to some dogmatic belief, but due to applying specific methods or solutions to a problem.

It is said that there are dozens of theories on creation in the scriptures! What does it show? The inner meaning and the intention of the scriptures is not merely to talk about how this world came about, but to negate the assumed reality of this world. So whenever the scriptures use a cause-effect discussion, it is just a method that will ultimately negate the absolute reality that is attributed to creation in its entirety! In his current state of development, the seeker believes in the reality of the world around him. So the scriptures and the seers use that as a starting point, and use his own burgeoning experience to unfold the greater Reality.

Before we delve into the methods and solutions that Advaita Vedanta utilizes, let us briefly look at the actual problem itself.

Ignorance: The Problem

The scriptures categorically say that the ignorance of our real nature as Pure Awareness, along with the resultant projection of this world of duality, is the core problem. When we see a snake in dim light we become petrified. The visions of a poisonous snake biting us is then swiftly followed by reactions like profuse sweating and a mortal fear for one's life. When a passerby then shines a flashlight, the assumed snake is realized to be a mere rope on the ground! Ignorance of the rope and the projection of a poisonous snake occurred simultaneously. This ignorance and its offshoots, like fear, sweating, etc., get destroyed in toto when light is leveled on the situation. Knowledge of the rope liberates the confused individual! Nothing else could have, which is why the scriptures unequivocally assert that *"knowledge alone liberates."*

Some objections may be raised here. For instance, had the confused person been endowed with faith in God, he would not have been afraid of the snake. But Advaita doesn't compromise, or conjecture. There is absolute clarity that knowledge alone will bestow freedom. What about beating the rope-snake with a stick? Would that save one? There is a humorous anecdote of a person coming upon his friend in a shocked state. When asked what transpired to cause this condition, the frightened friend replied that he came across a snake and picked up a stick to beat it. Unfortunately, it turned out to be a mere rope. "Why, then, are you shaken with fear?" asked the friend. To which he responded, "The stick which I picked up to beat the snake with turned out to be a snake!"

Knowledge Alone Liberates

Advaita Vedanta is firm on its stand that if ignorance is the problem, then knowledge alone can be the solution. In Acharya Shankara's seminal work, the *Vivekachudamani*, there is a verse which states:

mokshakaranasamagryam bhaktireva gariyasi

The verse above says that among all material aids for achieving *moksha*, liberation, bhakti or devotion is indeed the greatest. A perfunctory glance at this first line would make the dvaitin (dualist) jump with joy. "See! Your Acharya Shankara Himself claims that bhakti — as characterized by the duality of God and devotee — is the best means of achieving moksha." That would be their tall claim. The question is, how does Acharya Shankara define bhakti or devotion here? We see that definition in the very next line of the same verse:

svasvarupaanusandhanam bhaktirityabhidhiyate
Continuous contemplation of one's essential nature, svarupa, is indeed bhakti!

In other words, *nidhidhyasana* is the meaning here. The continuous contemplation of Vedic statements like *"Tat tvam asi – That thou art,"* obtained through a realized Guru, is the immediate cause. Since it produces direct realization it is said to be the greatest of all means. *Saguna bhakti,* or devotion to God with form, is a preparatory step which purifies the mind to be able to understand and assimilate the truth expounded by the Guru.

So how is this knowledge expounded?

Prakriyas, Scriptural Methods

The methods used by the scriptures to teach the ultimate truth, the substantive, are called *prakriyas*. These methods play a crucial role in unfolding the inner truth to the seeker and help in the dawning of the firm knowledge that obliterates ignorance and its offshoots. The *Mandukya Upanishad* uses the *avasthatraya prakriya*, the analysis of the three states of our every day experience. The *Taittiriya Upanishad* uses the *panchakosa prakriya*, the analysis of the five personality sheaths as it were. The right understanding of these methods and their usage is critical. Minus these scriptural methods it is impossible to arrive at this inner truth. Why is that? The seers are unequivocal in their assertion here. The subject matter of the scriptures, the Self, the *Atman,* is not available to sense perception. It is not an object to our eyes, ears, nose, etc. And if it is not an object of our direct sense perception, then any empirical study which relies on data gathered from direct perception will be of no use. Even inferential data relies on input derived from direct sense perception, so that is of no use as well.

Let's take the example of the panchakosa prakriya and see how it is used. The prakriya says that the Self is covered by the five sheaths of the human personality, namely, the *annamaya kosa,* the *pranamaya kosa,* the *manomaya kosa,* the *vijnanamaya kosa* and the *anandamaya kosa.* To unravel the Atman, these sheaths have to be removed. [See Nectar, Vol. #1]

The student may doubt here, and state; "You say that the Atman, the Self, is all-pervasive. Then you say it is covered by a sheath. So is the covering sheath bigger than the covered Self? If it is not, how will it cover the Self? And what is all-pervasive must also include the sheaths, or else it cannot be all-pervasive. How, then, are the sheaths removed to reveal the Atman?"

Why does this doubt arise? The student has, perhaps, imagined that the Atman, the Self, is an object, like a precious stone that is hidden inside five concentric cylindrical sheaths or covers. There is an outer annamaya kosa, then the pranamaya kosa is the next inner concentric cylinder, and so on. He also believes that he has to dive through these kosas into his heart or inner being to discover the hidden Self.

Let's dig a bit deeper with the example of annamaya kosa, the "food sheath," and see how it is used in the prakriya. There are three components here: *anna, maya,* and *kosa.* The word anna is straight forward. It means food. However, when we say annamaya, we may understand it to mean there is food everywhere! Why? The suffix, maya, in annamaya, can mean saturation, plenty, abundance, etc. For example, when we say *jalamaya,* we mean there is an abundance of water (*jala*) everywhere. Along the same lines, annamaya will come to mean "food everywhere." Not only that, we would have pasta, pancakes, and pizzas walking around everywhere! But that is not the case. Here, the suffix, maya, means *vikara,* or modification.

Therefore,

anna vikaratvat annamayah
It is annamaya because of modification of anna, or food.

Moreover, even the cause of this body, our parents, are also modifications of food — and their parents before them, and theirs, and so on. Since this body is created by food, sustained by food, and also ends up as food for others (animals, insects, fire, etc.), it is called annamaya. The beautiful and comprehensive work of Swami Vidyaranya, called the *Panchadashi,* also attests to this fact:

*pitrbhuktannjadviryajjato' nnenaiva vardhate dehah
so'nnamayah*
This body, that is born of the virility born of the food eaten by the parents, and grows by food only, is annamaya kosa....

Next, what does the word kosa mean? It should not be taken as a sheath only. The application here is:

kosavat acchadakatvat kosah
It is called a kosa because it hides or covers like a kosa.

The visualization here is of a sheath or a covering resembling that of a child being tucked into her bed with a warm blanket over her. The blanket is obviously much bigger than the tiny frame of the child, and hence the sleeping child can be completely covered by the blanket. Here it is different.

So how does this kosa operate? Imagine, if you will, that you are in a theater watching a new blockbuster movie. All the while you keep staring at the screen on which the movie is being shown. Yet your attention is always on the characters in the movie, the events therein, the emotions of the protagonists and the antagonists, the trials and tribulations etc., but never on the the screen on which the movie is taking place. The screen is all-pervading, that is, it is the very background on which the entire

> "Purusha, God, or Truth, transcends the world as we know it and is ever untouched by it. Acharya Shankara beautifully said, 'asango'ham, asango'ham, asango'ham puna puna — I am unattached, unattached, unattached again and again.' Advaitic Truth is beyond all conceptualization and dogma."

cinematic experience happens. Yet the projected movie seemingly covers the screen purely by diverting one's attention away from the screen — even while one is staring at it all the time. It does not actually cover the screen but it stands as though it is a covering!

Therefore, when we say *kosavat* — like a kosa, like a sheath, like a covering — then it becomes a prakriya, a way of wielding words, a method, a solution. If we say it is a kosa, then it means it is a sheath, and then the approach becomes a dogma or a school of thought or a philosophy.

Advaita Vedanta is also uncompromising on another fact. Even these prakriyas are not absolute truths. A lion in a dream frightens the dreamer, so much that he wakes up. Upon waking up, everything that transpired in the dream, including the lion, is realized to be an illusory experience. Nevertheless, the dream lion did serve the purpose of waking him up. In the same way, the right prakriya, when wielded correctly under the guidance of the compassionate Guru, wakes up the individual from this nightmarish samsara, the world of bondage.

In that sense, Advaita holds on to nothing. Absolutely nothing! There are no preferred methods or biases. The teacher chooses the methods and wields the words of the scriptures depending on the competency of the student. Both the pseudo-scientists and the pseudo-vedantins clutch at straws in the hope of making sense of what only seems to be. While the pseudo-scientist desperately tries to see things in the empirical light only, through the lens of data etc., the pseudo-vedantin becomes a rigid and dogmatic person who "dryly philosophizes" and only creates systems and concepts to explain his world view and idea of reality.

Advaita goes beyond these two. It uses methods, prakriyas, to teach the seeker the highest truth, and then very casually transcends those methods as well whenever appropriate. If Advaita was dogmatic, then there would exist a tight clinging onto these methods for their own sake, which is not seen at all. That independence is innate to Advaita Vedanta alone. The *Purusha Sukta* mantra boldly says, *atyatisthaddasangulam*. It means that the *Purusha,* or God, or Truth, transcends the world as we know it and is ever independent and untouched by it. No wonder Acharya Shankara beautifully said, "*asango'ham, asango'ham, asango'ham puna puna — I am unattached, unattached, unattached again and again.*" Advaitic Truth is beyond all conceptualization and dogma!

Futility of Actions in Securing Knowledge

We understand that there is a specific problem of bondage caused by ignorance. We also understand that the exact solution, *advaita jnana,* or non-dual knowledge, will liberate beings from ignorance. What about karma or actions? Well, they are of no great use, spiritually speaking. How can one say that? It is true, that actions can at least help purify one's mind when done with the right attitude, but they can never reveal the nature of the Eternal Subject, which in this case is the Self, the Atman. Acharya Shankara, himself, again reiterates that even millions of actions cannot reveal even a bit of the ultimate Truth. The *Mundaka Upanishad* also says, "*Examining the things secured by actions, let a seeker acquire detachment, for action can never secure for oneself what is not the effect of an action!*"

These statements, again, are not dogmas. Seekers can try out various paths and see if they work; the scriptures and seers never force anyone to follow them. But they definitely lay down a path and show the goal one could reach if that path were followed. Acharya Shankara, again, in His *Vivekachudamani,* says

moksasya kanksa yadi vai tavasti
If you desire liberation then do these.

If one says that one does not want liberation at all, well, no one will force it on an individual. The scriptural teaching is so comprehensive and compassionate in guiding the seeker that it graciously offers a blue print that is readily available for use along the path. Moreover, it has been tested and tried by not only the sages of ancient times, but also by innumerable seers of the modern times, like Sri Ramakrishna Paramahamsa and His disciple Swami Vivekananda, to quote just a couple of important names. Their exemplary lives, lived in recent times, have validated the scriptural means for us again and again.

Conclusion

The scriptures are not in the business of soul harvesting. If one wants to try some other path, one is very welcome to. But for Advaitic realization, only a round peg will fit a round hole. And that doesn't make it dogmatic, either. Even during the phase of seeking, called *sadhana,* the ancients have laid out the exact formula for preparing oneself to achieve the realization of Oneness. The four-fold qualification of discrimination, dispassion, the six mental attainments, and the desire for liberation, are sine qua non for Advaitic realization. And it all flows logically too [see chart on page 32].

Discrimination is defined as the separation of that which is real from that which is ephemeral. When one has successfully assimilated and understood what discrimination is, dispassion automatically follows. Why? No one will be interested in transient and painful objects. When dispassion dawns, then mind control, sense control, etc., naturally accrue to the individual. If one is not dispassionate, it follows that one has not discriminated enough. One cannot skip and compromise on these prerequisites. It is plain and simple. So what seems dogmatic is actually quite logical. What seems like an uncompromising stand is actually the perfect solution to our problems.

And only a seeker who really wants a solution to the problem of samsara will try it out. Mere coffee-table discussions and intellectual gymnastics will be of no use here. The spider's web irritates only when it comes in contact with one's eyes. All other parts of our body are not unduly disturbed or harmed when they come in contact with the web. In the same way, samsara or bondage is a problem to be solved only to a refined individual with a keen discriminative faculty. For others, it is not. They are oblivious, and will keep flitting from joy to sorrow and then back again, only to fall short of the goal. To a sincere seeker, the Guru appears and leads him or her back to the Source, which is unending bliss, by wielding the words of the scriptures and the methods laid out therein. After all, it is also the firm and uncompromising stand of our tradition that neither the scriptures nor the supreme Guru have anything more to gain. Whatever is being unfolded is purely for the sake of the disciple.

Shivakumar works for a start-up company that is setting up a chain of boutique resorts in India and South East Asia to promote Ayurveda, Yoga and Spirituality. He is also a novice student of Vedanta and guided by scholar-devotees of the Shankaracharya tradition of Sringeri in India.

Nirvanashatkam – Six Verses on Nirvana
by Shankara

AUM

I am neither mind, intelligence, ego, or chitta. Neither ears, nor tongue nor the senses of smell or sight; Nor am I ether, earth, fire, water, air:

I am Pure Consciousness and Bliss.
I am Shiva! I am Shiva!

I am neither the prana nor the five vital breaths. Neither the seven elements of the body nor its five sheathes. Nor hands nor fee nor tongue, nor the organs of sex or voiding.
I am Pure Consciousness and Bliss.
I am Shiva! I am Shiva!

Neither loathing nor liking have I, neither greed nor delusion; No sense have I of ego or pride, neither dharma nor moksha; Neither desires of the mind nor object for its desiring:
I am Pure Knowledge and Bliss.
I am Shiva! I am Shiva!

Neither right nor wrong doing am I, neither pleasure nor pain. nor the mantra, the sacred place, the Vedas, or the sacrifice; Neither the act of eating, the eater, nor the food:
I am Pure Consciousness and Bliss.
I am Shiva! I am Shiva!

Death nor fear I have none, nor any distinction of caste; Neither father nor mother, nor even a birth have I; Neither friend nor comrade, neither disciple nor guru:
I am Pure Consciousness and Bliss.
I am Shiva! I am Shiva!

I have no form or fancy, the all-pervading am I; Everywhere I exist, yet I am beyond the senses; Neither salvation am I, nor anything that can be known:
I am Pure Consciousness and Bliss.
I am Shiva! I am Shiva!

◆ *Swami Aseshananda*

FACING OUR FEAR
Placing Death in its Own Grave

Sitting and listening to Swami Aseshanandaji Maharaj giving discourses year to year, on every occasion, always gave one the sense of the likelihood of realization and transcendence being within one's grasp. Every so often he would utter that familiar refrain, *"We must make doubt doubt itself, make fear afraid of itself, and put death in its own grave."* Little did we know at the time, that as we grew in spirituality, we would be accomplishing exactly that by living life in the dharma and repeating the holy mantra granted by him. This transcription of one of his lectures, given in 1986, conveys his fiery and infectious spirit.

Our salutations to Him who is the truth of life and existence and whom the sages call by various names. Our salutations to Him whose glories are sung in sacred hymns of the various scriptures of the world, but whose limitless and infinite grandeur no mortal mind can comprehend. Our salutations to Him upon whom the devotees meditate in the shrine of their hearts, realizing an ineffable Presence in their deepest contemplations. May He illumine our understanding and prompt our minds to the path of Truth and Righteousness. May He reveal Himself unto our souls and dispel the gloom of illusion, fear, doubt, and darkness. Om Peace, Peace, Peace. Peace be unto us, Peace be unto all mankind. Hari Om Hari Om Hari Om Tat Sat

The Conquest of Fear

The subject of my talk today is "The Conquest of Fear." Western civilization is predominately a dualistic civilization. A dualistic civilization creates fear in the mind of the individual. Therefore, as long as the West thinks in terms of this dualism between man and God, fear will never disappear from the mind of the western man. Fear will disappear only when western man and western woman raises his or her consciousness to a higher level and realizes the truth that man in his true nature is infinite, not finite. Man is finite when he is ignorant. Man is infinite when he is illumined. And that is the reason why Swami Vivekananda came to the West and preached two doctrines: one, the Divinity of man; and second, the oneness of all existence. As long as you create a distinction between man and woman; as long as you feel the distinction between East and West; as long as you create a distinction between man and God, you will not be able to remove the presence of fear from your consciousness. Recently, a pamphlet came, and in that pamphlet is mentioned that Vedanta is preaching new theology. I do not agree. Theology is the gift of the West. Theology always teaches that man is finite. Vedanta insists that man is infinite.

Divine, not Sinful; Infinite, not Finite

Vedanta, as preached by Swami Vivekananda, tells the western man that his real nature is infinite and not finite; his real nature is Divine and not sinful; his real nature is perfect not imperfect. In one or two of his lectures on the concept of Evolution, Swami Vivekananda states, *"Evolution belongs to nature, perfection belongs to Spirit. Realize your true nature and be perfect."* Following him, then finally all your troubles will be over. Your long searches in temples and churches, in books and synagogues, will end. Man will have to make the return journey and find, to his great surprise, that He whom he searched for everywhere in the world, the nearest of the near, the dearest of the dear, is his very Self, is the very basis and background of his Consciousness; is his living Existence.

That is why Vedanta preaches only one thing: *Jivanmukti*. We have come here to earth to attain freedom. Freedom from what? Freedom from old age, disease, and death. Why are you afraid of death? Because you are ignorant. Because you identify yourself with your psycho-physical being, with your apparent self. All troubles will cease when you liquidate your ignorance and renounce your attachment to the flesh, attachment to your body/mind mechanism, and realize your infinite nature, your perfect nature, your immortal nature.

Harvest is Full, Revelers are Few

And that is the reason why *"the harvest is full but the revelers are few."* What do I mean by that? I mean that in order to realize your divinity you have to practice renunciation. What do we mean by renunciation? Renunciation means that you have to renounce your attachment to your psycho-physical being, and realize your true being to be Divine. When Swami Vivekananda came to this country and presented the Vedanta Philosophy, he opened his mouth in front of the assembly and declared: *"Ye divinities on earth, it is a sin to call a man sinner."* What is sin? Sin is only ignorance of one's Divine Nature, *Atman*. On account of your ignorance you attach yourself to your psycho-physical being. From *avidya*, ignorance, comes *asmita*, the sense of ego. Ego expresses itself in the form of attachment to the material things of life. What you see you think to be real; what you do not see, oh, it must be unreal. This inferior philosophy is called love of pleasure, love for power, love of wealth, love for the world. But the world constantly changes, is shifting sands. How can the world be real? Anything that changes is not real; that which does not change is Real.

And what is That which does not change? Surprise of surprises for the Westerner and the worldly, it is not your intellectual faculty of mind, but your Atman. It is your true Self, which is the principle of existence, the principle of knowledge, and the principle of bliss. When you think yourself to be a body/mind mechanism, you are a mere wave. But when you become illumined, you realize, "I am the ocean." *Chidananda rupah sivoham sivoham.* That means, *"I am the very form of Bliss; I am Siva, I am Siva."* Shankara was asked by his guru, "Who are you?" He did not answer, "I am a Brahmin coming from Malabar or Kerala." He said, *"Na mrityor na shanka.....I have no fear, I have no death, I am immortal. I am Existence Absolute, Knowledge Absolute, Bliss Absolute. I am ever free, never bound."*

Science and Philosophy Outstrip Theology

Therefore, in Vedanta, our best friends are not the theologians; our best friends are the scientists — especially great scientists like Schrodinger, when he writes in his book: *What is Life? Our experiences in consciousness are always singular, not dual or plural."* But western civilization has accepted dualism as the principle theme of life, as its main heritage. As I have mentioned before, western civilization is a compounded civilization of two streams of thought. The first stream of thought is called the Greek thought, championed by Plato and Aristotle. Plato has given idealism. He is the father of idealistic philosophy. Aristotle is the father of realistic philosophy. Or a better way of speaking would be to say that Plato is the father of philosophy and Aristotle is the father of science. Whatever it may be, reason is the supreme court of appeals there. But does not reason create a distinction between subject and object? It is therefore that Shankara states that the real seeker must transcend reason and realize his or her true nature. You are not a physical entity. Your are a spiritual being, which is timeless, which is deathless, which is changeless, which is infinite, and therefore perfect by nature.

The other day somebody asked me about that familiar statement, and, quoting from the Bible, said: *"God has created man in His image."* This is the voice of the theologian speaking. But Vedanta does not accept it, it is a relative truth only. The moment you think that you are created, you cannot think in terms of your immortality. And therefore, India introduces the nondual axiom of *Ajativada* to you — your birthless, deathless nature. Gaudapada speaks it in terms of noncausality. Meister Eckhart spoke about it too, that the real nature of man is uncreated Essence. But this was not accepted by the Catholic Church. The Catholic Church has accepted the thinking of Thomas Aquinas, and he has mentioned the natural and supernatural. "Natural" means reason. By reason you can prove the existence of God, but you cannot attain salvation without supernatural Grace.

So, whether you cite Augustine, or Thomas Aquinas, or modern theologians like Karl Barth and Paul Tillich, all of them were listening to one note only, the hypnotizing music of dualism; in other words, that man's real nature is finite.

But Swami Vivekananda, who preached Advaita Vedanta following the train of thought of the rishis of India, spoke about the real nature of man as being Infinite. Your real nature is unembodied, unfettered, unbounded Spirit. It is only on account of your self-hypnotization, your delimiting mind, your limited consciousness, that there is no chance of liquidating fear from the mind. Not through mere reasoning, or through thinking God to be separate from you, or via intellectually, but through personal experience of that exalted state of consciousness called Nirvikalpa Samadhi, will fear be destroyed and death placed in its own grave for all time.

Nondual Samadhi and Impersonal Reality

Therefore, you see before you on the podium, Sri Ramakrishna in a picture. This is a symbol, an expression of the state of consciousness which is called Nirvikalpa Samadhi. And there are other states of samadhi as well. In Savikalpa Samadhi, you enter communion with the personal God. That is fine. But in Nirvikalpa Samadhi you transcend the realm of the personal God and there is absolute identity between the *jivatman* and the *Paramatman*; between the individual soul and universal soul. And in order to realize this truth, a guru plays a very important part. A guru is not a man; guru is a state of consciousness. And that state of consciousness is timeless; that state of consciousness is nondual; that state of consciousness is the state which makes Advaita not a philosophy, but an experience.

Therefore, I am talking from the experience of Swami Vivekananda. Swami Vivekananda first experienced what we call God as Mother through the grace of Sri Ramakrishna. And his last experience was of God as Nirguna Brahman — God as impersonal, undifferentiated, universal, timeless, as well as changeless. Christ also experienced that.

But the West has come to interpret Christ's message in a dualistic way. I will not interpret Christ's message in a dualistic way. When Christ said, *"I and my Father are One,"* he had experienced Nirvikalpa Samadhi. Without the experience of Nirvikalpa Samadhi, one cannot rightly affirm that Atman and Brahman are one and the same. "I" is not the historical Jesus; "I" is the Atman Jesus. And "Father" is not the personal God, either. Theologians have ignorantly made the "Father" into the personal God. But I will not interpret the Father as the personal God. Father as God will convey to me the complete identity, absolute identity, between Atman, the true nature of mankind, and Brahman, Absolute Reality, that is Formless and Impersonal. Without attaining this ultimate Knowledge, *Advaita Jnanam*, fear will never disappear from your heart. You will be a prisoner of time, always thinking in terms of the future, of a post-mortem emancipation only, of going to heaven through the grace of God. Then you will think, "I will go and live there forever." You will never wake up and begin to think, "If there is the act of going, then there must also be an act of coming back."

"Coming and Going is all pure Delusion"

Thus, as Shankaracharya has said, when a person wants to go somewhere, what does it mean? Really, he only goes from his real Self to the non-Self, since all worlds are changing, thus unreal. And that is why Swami Vivekananda said, *"Coming and going is all pure delusion. The soul never comes nor goes. Where is the place to which it shall go, when all of space is in the soul? When shall be the time of entering or departing, when all time is in the soul?"*

Therefore, Advaita does not accept movement to be real. All movement is dreamlike. In the realm of relativity, Advaita accepts only one thing: discovery — discovery of the Truth which will make a person free from the tyranny of old age, disease, and death. It is past time for men and women to think not only in terms of manhood and womanhood, or a mere biological way of thinking, or historical way of thinking, but rather the Transcendental way of thinking. In other words, man and woman should think in terms of immortality, infinity, and uncreated nature. The moment you think that God created man, you break several laws of spirituality. Swamiji stated that it is not that God created man, but that man creates God in his mental image. A dualistic experience is when you are body conscious, But when you are conscious of your Atman, your real nature, that is a pure spiritual experience and then there is no distinction between the two.

Therefore, we do not think of identification with the personal God, we identify with the King, not the Prince. The personal God gets used as a means to satisfy your sense appetites. You take him with you down the path of the *Bhoga Marga*, the path of enjoyment. But Sri Ramakrishna did not accept the Bhoga Marga. He remained in Nirvikalpa Samadhi.

When I met Swami Turiyananda he quoted from Bhartrihari. *"In every enjoyment there is fear of disease."* You get a million dollars and there is fear of thieves. If you have achieved a very distinguished position, there is fear of competition. Take for example the Watergate incident. There is the fear of losing your status. You've built your house on sand. Why do we say sand? Because you've built your house on Time. Unless you are able to transcend time you will not be able to know the Truth. And in order to transcend time you must not move towards the periphery, you must move towards the center.

> "When a person wants to go somewhere, what does it mean? Really, he only goes from his real Self to the non-Self, since all worlds are changing, thus unreal. And that is why Swami Vivekananda said, 'Coming and going is all pure delusion. The soul never comes nor goes. Where is the place to which it shall go, when all of space is in the soul? When shall be the time of entering or departing, when all time is in the soul!'"

Because of fear, there is ignorance. And what is ignorance? Separation between man and man, between man and woman, between race and race, between religion and religion, between time and timelessness. Resting on the intellectual plane is not sufficient, nor the theological plane. Theology has given faith and Science has given reason, but both come under the category called *aparavidya*, lower knowledge. Why? Because when you use reason you are bound to bring time, space, and causation into the picture. Time, space, and causation are relative; that was the gift of Einstein. But Einstein did not accept Heisenberg's theory of indeterminacy. Heisenberg's theory, as well as Nagarjuna's theory called *shunyata*, and the theory of Gaudapada, *ajata*, are all very similar.

Christ, Gaudapada, Nagarjuna — Illumined Souls

But Heisenberg was not an illumined soul. Gaudapada was an illumined soul. Any kind of duality, however great, is born out of ignorance. When you become enlightened, you speak and act like the Christ. Christ's message was not a message of salvation; I call it a message of enlightenment. Salvation always conveys a postmortem emancipation idea. But freedom is *jivanmukti*, here and now. The Upanisads tell us that we must raise our consciousness from the intellectual plane to the spiritual plane and realize Nirguna Brahman. A clay mouse can never become one with a clay elephant; in manifestation there will be a difference. The personal God is in maya and is associated with time, space, and causation. Man is controlled by these three.

Purity and Renunciation

Where could you find it, this purity of the heart? Read in the Sermon on the Mount. What did he say? *"Be thee therefore perfect even as your Father who is in Heaven is perfect."* And what is the way? *"Blessed are the pure in heart, for they shall see God."* Purity of heart is not possible unless you accept the path of renunciation. Christ himself followed the path of renunciation. When I was studying in the Saint Paul's Cathedral Mission College in Calcutta, the Bible was compulsory. What did I learn from the Bible? I learned that *"Birds have nests, foxes have holes, but the son of man hath no where to lay his head."* Christ preached renunciation. And that is the reason why he told them, *"Leave behind your net and follow me. I will make you fishers of men."* When each young man came, they asked for a message. He told them to follow the commandments. Then Christ said, *"If thou wishest to be perfect, sell all thou hast and follow me."* What does this mean? Method. The method is renunciation. And Christ spoke against the Sadducees and Pharisees. But there is a brotherhood called the Essene brotherhood. It was a monastic brotherhood because it was the gift of Buddhism. Buddhism was in the Middle East, and the monks started a monastic order. It is a Buddhistically influenced brotherhood, what you call the Essene brotherhood. Some Jews also joined that brotherhood.

So Christ accepted monastic life. And therefore all his apostles are monks par excellence. Why become a monk? Because in order to be an ideal teacher you have to conserve your energy. We do not create energy; energy comes from food.

> "Western man accepts objective experience only. However, if you look, in meditation, behind the phenomenal universe, you will see the infinite Spirit, the Eternal Subject. And that will be possible only when you have accepted an illumined soul as your guru."

And we have to transmute that energy. Physical energy is to be transmuted into *Ojas*. And this must be stored up in the brain. Then alone you will be able to think about the eternal values of life, leaving the distractions alone.

And the most simplistic and eternal value is *Amrittatva*, immortality. Salvation is not immortality. If you want to attain salvation you will get a new body, as Paul has said — an incorruptible body. But immortality is all about Spirit; body is a limitation. The mind is constantly changing. Therefore, you must seek unlimited Consciousness, and unlimited Consciousness will come when you attain Nirvikalpa Samadhi.

In the *Brhadaranyaka Upanisad*, Yajnavalkya taught his wife, Maitreyi, spiritual principles. Maitreyi was not satisfied with money. *"Can one attain immortality through money? Can money bring immortality?" "No." "How can I realize my immortality?" "It is only through Atmajnana. Absolute Knowledge means realization of your real Self." "Then I want to learn."* That is why Yajnavalkya brought her the message of immortality. The rishis breathed it into the pages of the Upanisad. Every page speaks about immortality, of trying to be deathless, trying to be free from the tyranny of old age, disease, and death. Because dualism can spell disaster. It is only nondualism that will make you fearless; that is, will give you freedom from fear, freedom from death, freedom from loneliness, freedom from the anxieties of life.

An Exemplar, Please....

Recently, somebody asked me this question: "Swami, you have mentioned that life is a challenge. What is your challenge?" My challenge is that I want to teach western people a life of renunciation, a life of meditation, and also realizing immortality in this life with this body. Will you be able to succeed? I do not know. We shall try. If I do not succeed, the Master has told me: *"To work you have the right, but not to the fruits thereof."* What does it mean? It means you have to find an exemplar, one who has lived this life consciously.

Shankara was one such, though he lived only 32 years. I have lived this monastic life for more than 60 years now. But Shankara is outstanding. I have to say this, and I pay my homage. At first, when young, I use to think very highly of Plato. Plato's philosophy attracted me very much. But today, Plato's philosophy seems to be insignificant — childish compared to Shankara's philosophy, because Plato's philosophy is based on reason only. Shankara's philosophy is direct experience of God in an exalted state of Consciousness where there is no duality between man and God. It is this philosophy of Shankara that Swami Vivekananda preached in this country.

Some may say that the new theology of the day is going against Swamiji. If any person says that Vedanta is a new theology, he is not following the guideline set down by Shankara. And if any say that God created man in his image, that may be true for those people who accept theology to be the highest goal, but Vedanta does not accept this. The highest attainment of individual experience is nondual experience, where there is no distinction between the individual soul and the Universal Soul. In other words, your real nature is not finite, but infinite.

If you read the book called *Light of Asia,* in that book you will read about a dew drop entering the sea and getting lost; that means the individual merges in the Infinite. But *Nirvana* is interpreted as the "heaven of nothingness" by western scholars. But I do not interpret Nirvana as having anything to do with heaven or earth whatsoever. Nirvana is Brahman, and that means *"I and my Father are One,"* or I and my Mother are One. Are Father and Mother nothing, whether in heaven or not? Atman and Brahman are identical.

Western man accepts manifoldness in the universe to be real. As long as he accepts manifoldness to be real, he will not accept oneness of existence to be real. Shankara says that this Maya — *nama rupam* — name and form, constitute Maya. But the essence of Maya, and the background of Maya, is infinite Spirit. And there is no distinction between the real subject behind the psycho-physical being of man, and the real object behind the phenomenal universe. But it must ultimately be subjective, not objective experience. Western man accepts objective experience only. However, if you look, in meditation, behind the phenomenal universe, you will see the infinite Spirit, the Eternal Subject. And that will be possible only when you have accepted an illumined soul as your guru.

Jaya Vivekananda!

Swami Vivekananda was dissatisfied with the intellectual frame of reference, so he searched for his guru. He went to the Brahmo Samaj teacher, Devendranath Tagore. He only quoted the scriptures. But then he went to Sri Ramakrishna, and heard him say *"I have seen God in samadhi."* He told him that in savikalpa samadhi one enters communion with the personal God. In nirvikalpa samadhi one attains absolute identity with the impersonal God, the Godhead, the Ground of Existence. And Sri Ramakrishna told him, *"If you want to realize God I will teach you."* Then he sat at the feet of the Master. And what did the Master do? Just what Christ or any illumined soul will do, raise the disciple's consciousness from the intellectual frame of reference to the spiritual frame. And in the spiritual frame of reference there are those two states. When you maintain the pure ego, you attain the personal aspect of God. When you transcend your pure ego and realize the Atman, there is absolute oneness, there is absolute identity.

> "So it is here, you see, that abhayam — fearlessness — comes. It is when you accept three things: first, the advaita; second, guru shakti; third, the concept of God as Mother. That has nothing to do with masculine, feminine, or neuter. The concept of God as Mother is relatively unknown to the West."

My subject here is *abhaya,* fearlessness. And so I ask you, how can there be sorrow, how can there be evolution, how can there be fear, if one has raised his consciousness to a plane where there is no duality, where there is only absolute identity between the individual soul and the Universal Soul. To realize this, sadhana is necessary, meditation is necessary. You have to hear from an illumined soul. Who is an illumined soul? That one who has realized God in Savikalpa Samadhi, as well as the nondual Spirit of God in Nirvikalpa Samadhi.

Sri Ramakrishna

So here you'll find Sri Ramakrishna. Sri Ramakrishna's God-consciousness was right in the palm of his hand. That which is night to most beings, is daytime to the knowers of Truth. *Brahmajnana,* God-consciousness, is the daytime of Sri Ramakrishna. If you accept Sri Ramakrishna, bend all your efforts for that one end, everything will change and pass away, but God will not change and pass away. Realize God. And it is not just a concept or idea. A concept or idea will not change your character. Your character will be changed when you become dissatisfied with the status quo of the world. The world is changeful. That is why Krishna calls it *anityam* and *asukam,* noneternal and full of suffering. All worldly experiences will be reduced into dust and ashes when death knocks at the door. But a man need not be afraid if he has led a pure life, a spiritual life, if he has a guru to fortify his faith, strengthen his conviction, and to protect him from all dangers and difficulties of life. Here, the image of Holy Mother comes to my mind.

Sri Sarada Devi — God as Mother

When I came to the West, it was the Holy Mother's voice that said, *"I will protect you from all danger and difficulties."* It's like a mother bird protecting the fledgling. *"Don't be afraid. You have seen me and I will be the monitor of the soul and the awakener of your spiritual consciousness."* It was my service of Swami Saradananda that brought to my consciousness that Holy Mother was not just a saintly human, but the Divine Mother herself. After my initiation with Her, I said to Swami Saradananda, "Maharaj, please give me a method, because Holy Mother has not given any method." He did not scold me much, but that time he said, *"You are a great fool! The mantra has been given to you by Her, and that is the last word of spiritual life. Cling to Her Feet and create Her image in your heart. And bend all your efforts to follow the method given by Her. Then you will be able to reach the goal through the goodness of time."*

So it is here, you see, that *abhayam* — fearlessness — comes. It is when you accept three things: first, the advaita; second, guru shakti; third, the concept of God as Mother. That has nothing to do with masculine, feminine, or neuter. The concept of God as Mother is relatively unknown to the West. But I have studied and I have reflected on that. It is the concept of God which has bridged the gulf between the advaita of Shankara and monotheism of St. Augustine. It is the concept of God as Mother which has bridged the gulf between Nirguna Brahman and Saguna Brahman, the personal God and impersonal God. When you worship, you think of God as Mother; that means the personal aspect of God. When you attain Nirvikalpa Samadhi, Mother remains in Her true nature as Nirguna Brahman.

A worshiper of Divine Mother has the vision of Mother in the personal aspect. And also *Aham Devi* — I am one with the Devi. That means I am Brahman, Nirguna Brahman. Sri Ramakrishna also had the vision of the Mother, you see, when he was practicing dualistic sadhana. In the beginning of his advaita sadhana, he still held a bhakti form of the Mother. Then he reached Oneness and attained the transcendent realm. That is also Swami Vivekananda's experience of Nirvikalpa Samadhi.

Swami Vivekananda

The Impersonal may become personal. When I am one, I want to become many. But when you transcend the realm of the personal God, that is called *shunya.* Shunya means void — void of name, form, quality, and attributes. It cannot be expressed in language. It is only a person who has experienced Nirvikalpa Samadhi who will know it, will feel it, and will live by it all through the days of his blessed life.

So that is the reason why we love Swami Vivekananda. Swami Vivekananda is the awakener of the consciousness of the American people. By reading Swami Vivekananda you will learn what self-confidence, self-reverence, self-awakening are all about. You are asleep. You are frittering away what energies you have via veiled pursuits in this mundane, material world. Now bend all your efforts towards realizing the Truth which will make you free. If any civilization cannot produce an illumined soul, that civilization has failed from the religious point of view.

Swami Vivekananda and Vedanta have come to initiate or introduce the western man and woman to a higher value of life which will bring self-confidence, purity of heart, nobility of character, and also a universal outlook towards the world and its beings. Deification of the world is only possible when one becomes illumined. And afterwards what happens is compassion; just like Buddha, you attain Nirvana. And after Nirvana he accepted the bodhisattva idea. He retraced his steps from the throne of nirvana and vowed that as long as there is one soul left suffering he would not merge and disappear. Similarly, you will find in our order that Swami Vivekananda has given the maxim, *atmano mokshartham jagad dhitaya cha* — first you have to be enlightened, and then you can help to save suffering souls.

So bend all your efforts for the good of all, for the happiness of all, by setting an example. You cannot do good to people, you can only do good to yourself. I have withdrawn my mind from the thought that I can do good. I only live the divine life, and those who want to learn it come and ask questions. I answer in my own way. But your real teacher is within, you see. Find your real teacher, the God within, and He will teach you, and his teaching will never fail. He will never disappoint you. And therefore, the method is very important. The method is renunciation. The method is meditation.

The West has given too much emphasis on individual ego, and it loves power and greed. When you meet a person in this country you always ask, "How do you do?" The ego responds, "I do everything," but the Atman remains silent, knowing it does nothing. It reminds me of Swami Turiyananda when he came to your country. One devotee said, "Swami, there must be some inner meaning to life." Then he entered into a discourse on the Vedanta philosophy. He explained, "When we see any person with these eyes, that is called the name and form. But when your vision is clear, you see through name and form and behold only the Essence. Name and form belong to maya. Essence belongs to God. Name and form are bound to nature. God is boundless. Therefore, you cannot serve two Gods.

Become Fearless and Find Freedom

So become fearless and find Freedom. You will attain immortality. You will attain perfection. Vedanta does not ask that you give up anything. Just ask this question again and again: "Who am I? Who am I? Who am I?" And when you have experienced the Truth of God, and give up what other people think of you, you will say, "I am the eternal Spirit. I am the infinite Ocean. I am the perfect Being. I am the immortal Soul." And that we find represented in this age by Sri Ramakrishna as well as Holy Mother.

Therefore, I bow down in reverence to Holy Mother. May She Bless me. Because a real teacher of religion must be a knower of Truth who has experienced the Truth. It is when you have experienced the Truth in Nirvikalpa Samadhi that you are able to preach Advaita. Advaita is not a theology. Advaita is an experience in Nirvikalpa Samadhi where there is no duality between Atman and Brahman. That one is the one who has realized *Aham Brahmasmi* — I am Brahman."

The guru gives the mantra *Tattvamasi*, Thou art That, and the shishya, the disciple, through hard work and tremendous enthusiasm, reaches Nirvikalpa Samadhi. It happened in the case of Swami Vivekananda. Sri Ramakrishna gave Tattvamasi, and told him, "You are Divine, you are Perfect." Then, in Cossipore garden, he meditated and his mind transcended the realm of the personal God. Then Swamiji said, *"The void has entered the void,"* He meant that his experience went beyond thought, beyond speech, beyond comprehension of the finite mind. And the truth is, that he alone knows who has experienced It in the depth of his consciousness, in the shrine of his heart, in the sanctuary of his soul.

So, Vedanta is an experience. And this experience will transform life, will edify character, and grant noble vision. It will transform an individual soul into a illumined soul. And for this, we present to you Sri Ramakrishna, who is the Great Master, who loves us, who draws our attention just like an ocean drawing the attention of the river. The river will never stop until it meets the ocean. Similarly, the soul is like a river. It is moving towards the goal. And the goal is perfection, the goal is immortality, the goal is *jivanmukti*.

And that immortality can be attained only when you have realized that your true nature is not finite, but infinite. Your true nature is not mortal, but immortal. Your true nature is not imperfect, but perfect. Yours is the oneness of existence. You enter into diversity when you think of this relative world. But absolute oneness, absolute identity — that which will remove all fears from your heart — removes the mirage of this world. And then the knots of your heart will be cut asunder. All the doubts will be broken into shreds when man sees God as the very Life of his life, as the very Soul of his soul, as the very Spirit of pure Existence.

It is this Spirit that causes the mind to think and the body to live. This spirit is Yogic fire. When it burns, the mind and body will be transcended, and you will become illumined. Where will your fear be then?

Swami Aseshananda, a direct disciple of Sri Sarada Devi, Sri Ramakrishna's wife and spiritual consort, was the Spiritual Minister of the Vedanta Society of Portland for over forty years. He also received holy company with some of the direct disciples of the Great Master. He is the author of *Glimpses of a Great Soul*, on the life and teachings of Swami Saradananda.

WE ARE ATMAN ALL-ABIDING

108 Verses on The Atman

Atman — The Eternal Essence of Consciousness, pervading everything

1) Here I sit in deep reflection
   Witnessing the mind's dejection
   News has reached our distraught ears
   Focusing unspoken fears

2.) My dear friend they say is dying
   He is weeping, I am crying
   In the end despite these tidings
   We are Atman all-abiding

3) I pace the floor and wring my hands
   Leave footprints in nocturnal sands
   Midnight oil is long consumed
   Incense gone, the air perfumed

4) Who am I and what is real?
   Eyes which see and hands which feel?
   Elements and realm of senses?
   Vital force, the mind's pretenses?

5) Suddenly with thoughts transported
   Negativity aborted
   Vanished futile speculation
   Gone all lines of demarcation

6) Answers come with lightning speed
   Mind is calm, heart pays heed
   Mother works Her magic deftly
   Realization seeps in swiftly

7) We are not the body gown
   Nor the life-force winding down
   Never mental cogitation
   Pleasure-seeking occupation

8) Body dotes on sense perception
   Mind indulges thought projection
   Vital sheath is passion bound
   Midst these, Atman can't be found

9) Say farewell to wife and husband
   Parents, children, all your loved ones
   None of them can ever part, for
   Atman dwells within the heart

10) Atman neither comes nor goes
    Cannot think but always knows
    Can't be stilled or set in motion
    Vast and free like boundless ocean

11) This called Atman never dies
    Say the wisest of the wise
    They should know, yet knowing nothing
    Are they mocking, merely bluffing?

12) Logic, rationale and reason
    Mix in heart to lightly season
    Taste the triple Atman blended
    Inner, outer and transcendent

13) Name and form are outer Atman
    Mind and thought the inner Atman
    Intellect and nature lacking
    Seek Paramatman all-attracting

14) Merge with Atman free from dying
    Ever leading, never vying
    Always witness, pure detachment
    Veiled from those with sense-attachment

15) Death defying, always living
    Free from taking and from giving
    Past all hope of understanding
    Intellect notwithstanding

16) Far beyond the mental knower
    Soaring higher, creeping lower
    Never caught in wise conception
    Is the Atman—pure perception

17) Glimpsed, they say, with inner vision
    Lost at once through indecision
    There again when least expected
    Gone when ego is detected

18) Not affected, never changing
    Self-effulgent, thought engaging
    Lights the land of Pure Awareness
    Timeless, deathless, causeless, fearless

19) Ever free and never bound
    Never lost yet seldom found
    Vast and timeless, all-pervasive
    Everywhere yet most evasive

20) Growth It never undergoes
    Illness, sadness, weal or woes
    Nor expansion nor contraction
    Nor reflection nor refraction

21) Ever lit in Self-effulgence
    Lights the sun without indulgence
    Free from taint and ever stainless
    Breathless, endless, voidless, gainless

22) Void of either friend or foe
    Sets the universe aglow
    On Its surface all reflected
    But the Atman, unaffected

23) Not described for fear of flawing
    Teachers silent, hemming, hawing
    Seekers lost in rapt attention
    Barely breathing, loath to mention

24) Atman, then, escapes detection
    Philosophical dissection
    Thought and speech fall back in awe
    Atman transcends Cosmic Law

25) Homogenous, forever full
    Partless, indivisible
    Continuous, inseparable
    Mindless, inconceivable

26) Never fooled by false illusion
    Imposition, mass delusion
    Cognizant without a mind
    Nothing present there to bind

27) Essence of eternal life
    Draws the husband to the wife
    For Its sake the child is loved
    By Its grace, the Gods above

28) Seeking, failing, or attaining
    Gaining, losing, waxing, waning
    Atman is beyond all these
    Sovereign Lord of all It sees

29) Witness of the Universe
    With no second, always first
    Can't be one or fleeting few
    Void of many or of two

30) Atman is devoid of gender
    Firm detachment ever tender
    Forms the ground of Unity
    For profuse diversity

31) Atman infills everything
    Causes hearts to take to wing
    Colors sky and ocean blue
    Steeped in bliss, through and through

32) Has no equal here or there
    All-pervasive, everywhere
    Can't possess It, cannot lose
    Selects only whom It would choose

33) Not a human or celestial
    Never known by creature bestial
    Yet informs all living things
    Nature, workers, warriors, kings

34) Glimpsed in deepest meditation
    Far beyond this dream creation
    Some describe as boundless Light
    Others as effulgent night

35) Some there are who hear of It
    Others live in fear of It
    Rare the few abiding there
    Many those who do not care

36) Atman, formed of primal Essence
    Omnipresent, conscious nescience
    Lacking naught but holding nothing
    Ever full, devoid of stuffing

37) Egoless and formless, faceless
    To the mind completely traceless
    Staring out of eyes in faces
    Unbeknownst in most all cases

38) Never stained by false impressions
    Evil, vice or past regressions
    Purity without a taint
    Sought by wise one, sage and saint

39) Outstrips all that swiftly run
    Turns insipid earthly fun
    Pain and pleasure bend a knee
    Worship equanimity

40) Not deterred by walls and doors
    Not contained by ceilings, floors
    Time and space pose no restriction
    Thought and deed create no friction

41) Matchless, irrepressible
    Massive, infinitesimal
    Occupies abundant space
    Everywhere but leaves no trace

42) Said to be our inmost being
    Immanent, completely freeing
    Spark of Brahman in the heart
    Never split or drawn apart

43) Not destroyed and never killed
    Never emptied, never filled
    Not perceived with mind and senses
    Not perceived the mind grows pensive

44) Never righteous or defiling
    Immaculate and all-beguiling
    Ancient yet forever young
    Praised by all with glories sung

45) There in waking, dreaming, sleeping
    Watching others sowing, reaping
    Those who know the Self in all
    Never fear, never fall

46) They are joyful, never pining
    Like the sun that's always shining
    Those whose refuge is the Self
    Live in peace and no one else

47) Unseen fragrance from a flower
    Wood possessing fire's power
    Water present in the ice
    Whitish color in the rice

48) Subtle like these bare depictions
    Futile to engage description
    Trying makes my tongue go dead
    Kali steps upon my head

49) Even so, in sacred scripture
    Sages paint a glowing picture
    Seek the Atman, all declare
    Only world-renouncers dare

50) Jesus, Buddha, Moses, Krishna
    Mohammed and Mahavishnu
    All united in the Truth
    Atman is the final proof

51) Upanishads and Vedas, Gita
    Manifest as Rama, Sita
    Radhe sister knew It well
    Saved Arjuna from his hell

52) Once perceived by Rishis old
    Passed to child and seekers bold
    Kept alive by teachers brave
    Shiva in His mountain cave

53) Thus came down through countless ages
    Ever one but viewed in stages
    Recently was Gadadhar
    Swamiji and Sarada

54) Prayer wheels forever turning
    Rosaries, with faith discerning
    Temples, circumambulation
    Millions bow in full prostration

55) Millions plunged in ignorance
    Will they ever be convinced?
    End all racial genocide
    And this spiritual suicide

56) Ultimately all will see It
    Identify, immerse and be It
    What a heady revelation
    Kali Ma in jubilation

57) 'Tis the Atman all revere
    Loving It yet full of fear
    Caught in individuation
    Clinging to this human station

58) Shake them up, O awesome Mother
    Strip from them this Maya cover
    Show them mighty conflagrations
    Shattered cities, death of nations

59) Famines, floods, plagues, diseases
    Cracking earth and modern Caesars
    Tidal waves destruction bound
    Lava flows dissolving towns

60) In the end a fresh vibration
    With this seed a new creation
    Wind of breath on primal essence
    Breeding subtle life-quintessence

61) Cosmic play begins anew
    First with one, then with two
    Come the many, life is teeming
    Mass collective mental dreaming

62) Mundane dreams and dreams essential
    Dreams of bliss and nightmare central
    Dreams of bondage, dreams of freedom
    Dreams exciting, dreams of tedium

63) Dreams forsake, from bonds be free
    Know the Truth and clearly see
    Here is Atman all around
    Blissful Atman flowing down

64) Brooding mind must make a shift
    Strip the wrappings off the gift
    One by one the layers fall
    Atman none of them at all

65) Not the life-force, not the flesh
    Nor the thinking consciousness
    Not the body or the birth
    Fire, water, air or earth

66) Not the ego's joys and sorrows
    Intellect or light it borrows
    Eyes or sight, tongue or taste
    Hands or feet, hair or face

67) Not the act of procreation
    Nor the flow of nerve sensation
    Not a set of mind impressions
    Doubt, despair or deep depressions

68) Light of Atman all aglow
    Wisdom path for all that know
    Be this Light, prepare the way
    Live as Atman every day

69) Sun still shines though clouds may hide it
    Stars still sparkle there despite it
    Quite like this the Self remains
    Though ignorance may cloud the brain

70) Fiery sun repels the night
    Darkness never mars its light
    Similar the Self resplendent
    Though It shines within, transcendent

71) Light of stars and glowing moon
    Brilliant fire and sun at noon
    Firefly, lightning intense
    None can match Its radiance

72) Nothing luminous compares
    Lesser lights or distant glares
    Other lights are mere reflections
    All included, no exceptions

73) Light of Self is Pure Being
    Pure knowing, perfect seeing
    Truth and Bliss and Peace and Love
    Grace within, without, above

74) Those who seek It must be fearless
   With regards to Spirit, peerless
   Simple, honest, patient, striving
   All committed, sense depriving

75) Same to all in sentiment
   Firm, of equal temperament
   Sensitive and all-detaching
   Loving Truth, the rest dispatching

76) Pure despite all impositions
   Tainted not by vile conditions
   Passions, sorrows, come what may
   Atman keeps them all at bay

77) Atman is immediate
   Practical, expedient
   Nothing forces It apart
   Dwells at peace within the heart

78) Ancient yet with lasting youth
   Hiding nothing false, all Truth
   Seeking It for many lives
   Beings finally realize

79) Atman does not need a mantra
   Can't be had by rites or Tantra
   Merged in one infinity
   Spiritual epitome

80) Universe shines undivided
   Play of Maya, many-sided
   Neither sees the Self unborn
   Pure, resplendent, light adorned

81) Has no guide, imparts no teaching
   Grace imbued and Truth far-reaching
   Wonderful yet free from wonder
   Bursts all ignorance asunder

82) How to know this great Protector?
   Method, path and true preceptor
   Sacrifice and self-surrender
   Kill the ego, foul pretender

83) Let this Force tear mind apart
   Witness dual thoughts depart
   Fix one-pointed inward gaze
   Burn away obscuring haze

84) Catch a glimpse of Atman's brilliance
   Captivating Soul-resilience
   Dwell awhile in subtle spheres
   Alien to hopes and fears

85) Lose the taste for worldly pleasure
   Selfish acts, terrestrial treasures
   Infinite frivolities
   Harmful immoralities

86) Find the purpose for existence
   Storm the gates with firm insistence
   Weakness is a bane to progress
   Without effort life proves fruitless

87) Grace and effort hand in hand
   Indicate the master plan
   Striving is the key to knowing
   Wind of Grace is always blowing

88) Blazing sun is always glowing
   Mighty rivers ever flowing
   Ethers fill infinity
   Mountains stand eternally

89) Vaster than the boundless void
   Subtler than the primal word
   Constant as the northern star
   Atman is supreme by far

90) Unthinkable this tragedy
   Forgetting Atman's majesty
   Grasping matter, losing Grace
   Strange indeed this human race

91) Materialist philosophy
   Mental mediocrity
   Cultures steeped in fad and fashion
   Churches mad with money passion

92) Trapped amidst their fine possessions
   Stamped upon their mind's impressions
   And their hopeful expectation
   Postmortem emancipation

93) Land of honey, streets of gold
    Endless riches there to hold
    End to pain, increase of pleasure
    Joy of everlasting leisure

94) Atman knowers do not care
    For exquisite pleasures rare
    Contemplating something higher
    Cheating death, that baneful liar

95) Atman lovers recognize
    Earthly life demands a price
    Just as name and form exist
    So will joy and pain persist

96) Therefore, they are set at ease
    Hearts in love and minds at peace
    Happy and forever free
    In transcendent Unity

97) Join this band of Soul ecstatics
    Leave the land of blind erratics
    Rise and live the life Divine
    Free of I and me and mine

98) Ego is an imposition
    Name and form a tense condition
    Universe a magic theater
    Seemingly bereft of leader

99) Good and bad are chains that hold
    One of iron, one of gold
    Time and space are rivers flowing
    Never ending, never knowing

100) Discriminate my precious friend
     Cause this paradox to end
     Know for sure once and for all
     Spirit rises, matter falls

101) Once you've learned this final lesson
     Take the Mother's precious blessing
     Refuge in the Blessed Lord
     Death destroying Wisdom-Sword

102) Shakti power improvising
     Kundalini waking, rising
     Deftly wielding Mother's force
     Journey to your primal Source

103) Perennial, this timeless fountain
     Streaming down from sacred mountain
     Feel the Soul's exhilaration
     Unconditioned liberation

104) Graced with body or beyond
     You are Atman free of bonds
     Doubt of this is mind pollution
     Therefore teach this bold solution

105) Chanting, serving, contemplation
     Japa mala, meditation
     Simple, honest, truthful pleasure
     Meaningful beyond all measure

106) Happy love of lonely study
     Talks of God with bosom buddy
     Worship of the Chosen One
     No devotions left undone

107) Now I've broached this subject bold
     One-o-eight if all are told
     Speaking thus on one condition
     That the Self defies description

108) So be silent, peaceful, still
     Offer all to higher Will
     All immersed in bliss sublime
     This is Atman, Truth Divine

Babaji Bob Kindler, February, 1995

For Lex Hixon, Ramakrishnadas Baul,
my dear spiritual brother
and precious companion

SRV Associations — Babaji's Teaching Schedule, 2014

SRV Hawai'i
Administrative Office
PO Box 1364
Honoka'a, HI 96727

SRV Associations
website: www.srv.org
email: srvinfo@srv.org
Phone: 808-990-3354

SRV Oregon
1922 SE 42nd Ave.,
Portland, OR 97215
Ph: 503-774-2410

SRV San Francisco
465 Brussels Street
San Francisco, CA 94134
Ph: 415-468-4680

February/March, 2014

SRV San Francisco (Meditation, 6 to 7 am)
2/14 Fri 7:00pm Arati/Satsang
2/15 Sat 9:30am Class: Upanisads
            7:00pm **Sri Ramakrishna Birth Puja** (solar)
2/16 Sun 9:30am Class: Upanisads

SRV Oregon (Call for meditation times)
2/21 Fri 6:00 pm Book Signing and Talk with Babaji
                    At Opening To Life, 407 NE 12th
2/22 Sat 9:30am Class: Upanisads
            6:00pm **Sri Ramakrishna Birth Puja** (solar)
2/23 Sun 9:30am Class: Upanisads
2/26 Wed 7:00pm Meditation & Scripture Class
2/27 - 3/2 — Sivaratri Retreat

Sivaratri Retreat, Feb 27 - March 2
Subject: Sri Sivanam Sankirtanam
Location: Seattle, WA
(arrive Thursday night, depart Sunday at noon)

3/7 Fri 7:00pm Satsang with Babaji
3/8 Sat 9:30am Class: Upanisads
          6:00pm SRV Puja, Siva Puja
3/9 Sun 9:30am Upanisads

May, 2014

SRV San Francisco (Meditation, 6 to 7 am)
5/9   Fri 7:00pm Arati/Satsang
5/10 Sat 9:30am Class: Shankara & the Upanisads
            7:00pm SRV Puja
5/11 Sun 9:30am Class: Divine Mother Teachings

SRV Oregon (Call for meditation times)
5/16 Fri 7:00pm Satsang with Babaji
5/17 Sat 9:30am Class: Teachings of the Buddha
            6:00pm SRV Puja, Siva Puja
5/18 Sun 9:30am Class: Upanisads
5/21 Wed 7:00pm Meditation & Scripture Class
5/22 - 26 — SRV Spring Retreat

Memorial Day Weekend Retreat, May 22 - 26
Subject: (Another foray into) Gaudapada's Karika
Location: Windwood Waters (Wind River Region)
(arrive Thursday evening, depart Monday at noon)

July, 2014

SRV San Francisco (Meditation, 6 to 7 am)
7/3 Thu SRV SF Summer Retreat Begins

**SRV American River Retreat
over Independence Day, July 3 - 9**
Subject: The Life & Teachings of Swami Vivekananda

SRV Oregon (Call for meditation times)
7/12 Sat 9:30am Class: Upanisads
            6:00pm **Guru Purnima Puja**
7/13 Sun 9:30am Class: Upanisads
7/16 Wed 7:00pm Meditation & Scripture Class
7/18 Fri 6:00 pm Satsang with Babaji
7/19 Sat 9:30 am Class: Upanisads
            6:00pm SRV Puja, Siva Puja
7/20 Sun 9:30 am Class: Upanisads
7/23 Wed 7:00pm Meditation & Scripture Class
7/26 - 27 — SRV Portland Seminar

SRV Weekend Seminar, July 26 - 27
Subject: Sri Krishna's Timeless Message

September/October 2014

SRV San Francisco (Meditation, 6 to 7 am)
9/25 Thu 7:00pm Arati/Satsang
9/26 Fri 7:00pm Arati/Satsang
9/27 Sat 9:30am Class: Divine Mother Teachings
            7:00pm **Durga Puja**
9/28 Sun 9:30am Class: Divine Mother Teachings

SRV Oregon (Call for meditation times)
10/3 Fri 7:00pm Satsang with Babaji
10/4 Sat 9:30am Divine Mother Teachings
            6:00pm **Durga Puja**
10/5 Sun 9:30am Divine Mother Teachings
10/8 Wed 7:00pm Meditation & Scripture Class
10/9 - 10/13 — SRV Navaratri Retreat

**SRV Kali Durga Navaratri Retreat
Discoverer's Day Weekend, October 9 - 13**
Subject: Prana and the Illusion of Death
Location: Windwood Waters (Wind River Region)

10/15 Wed 7:00pm Meditation & Scripture Class
10/18 Sat 9:30am Class: Upanisads
            6:00pm SRV Puja, Siva Puja
10/19 Sun 9:30pm Class: Upanisads

*** Vedanta for Teens & Children: at SRV Oregon and SRV San Francisco
Contact Annapurna Sarada — Ph: 808-990-3354**

See retreat details on pg.58 or visit www.srv.org ▪ Livestreamed Weekend Classes, 9:30am to 12:30pm PST

SRV Associations — Babaji's Teaching Schedule, 2014
SRV Hawaii Ashram, Big Island

Sunday Live Streaming Classes, 2:30 - 5:30pm
Directions: Call: 808-990-3354

Jan 12, 19, 26, & Feb 2, 2014
Shakta-advaita-vada II

March 23, 30, & April 6, 13, 20, 27
Dissolving the Mindstream

June 8, 15, 22
Sankhya Yoga

August 10, 17, 24, 31, & September 7, 14
Bhagavad Gita

Nov 2, 9, 16, 23, 30, & Dec TBA
Prana and the Illusion of Death

Notice:
Our 2014 schedule is subject to change.
Please check the calendar on our website
www.srv.org
and sign our e-list at classes for notifications
or read our e-newsletter, Mundamala.
You can also contact your local SRV center:
Hawaii & Oregon: 808-990-3354
San Francisco: 415-468-4680

Check www.srv.org for Hawaii retreats
or see our Retreats Pages in the back of this issue

Sign up for:
- SRV Magazine: Nectar of Non-Dual Truth
- Raja Yoga email study with Babaji
- SRV's Facebook page
- SRV's YouTube channel: Teaching videos
- Godblogs: Inspired Dialog

* Please call or inquire about our Children's Classes
Contact Annapurna Sarada — Phone 808-990-3354

SRV Hawai'i Administrative Office
PO Box 1364
Honoka'a, HI 96727
Ph: 808-990-3354

SRV Associations' website:
www.srv.org
email:
srvinfo@srv.org

Checkout SRV on Facebook: facebook.com/srv.vedanta

SRV Associations Website
www.srv.org
srvinfo@srv.org

SRV On The Web
Visit www.srv.org to find:

SRV's Livestream Channel
Webcast Time Zone Schedule
SRV's YouTube Channel Class Series
- Advaita of the Avatars
- Devotion of Nonseparation
- The Wisdom Particle
- Non-Touch Yoga

Explore our Website links to find:
- Sanskrit Chants to learn/practice
- Devotional Songs
- Audio Discourses

Teachings:
- Articles
- Raja Yoga Sutras Study
- SRV's Teachings for Youth/Children
- Podcasts

Magazine:
- View our online archive of Nectar
- Order back issues of Nectar

News & Events
- Mundamala – SRV's e-newsletter
  Full of teachings and more

SRV Associations — Retreats for 2014

Sivaratri Retreat
February 27 – March 2, 2014, Seattle WA

Gathering in February over the auspicious time of Sivaratri, the SRV Associations and its members, students, and initiates will meet to worship the Lord of Wisdom, and to sing and study the Sivanam Sankirtanam together. Through recitation, chanting, study, and memorization — i.e., svadhyaya — the truths of religion and philosophy get imprinted in both the subtle and causal memory, leaving a beneficial atmosphere there. At this retreat, a hands-on participation in both chanting, finding, and contemplating the meaning of Sanskrit words and slokas will form the emphasis.

"A tiger skin around His handsome body, His cosmic dance astounds His legions. Transported they watch as writhing snakes and disheveled hair swirl around a graceful neck garlanded with skulls. Light from the crescent moon on His brow enhances the enthralling scene."

–Tulsidas

Text: *Sri Sivanam Sankirtanam (and other stotrams)*
Location: Seattle, Washington
Arrival: Thursday, February 27, after dinner and by 10:00pm
Departure: Sunday, March 2nd, at 12:00pm (approximately)
Tuition (all inclusive): $275; students $137   **Registration:** Starts now. Tuition is due by **Feb 14th**
Financial hardship?   Call 808-990-3354 to discuss options
Register by email: srvinfo@srv.org or by phone 808-990-3354

The Stunning Insights of Gaudapada's Karika
May 22 – 26, 2014, Wind River region, WA

In and throughout the vast sweep of Indian philosophy and religion there is scarcely anything as profound and elevating as Advaita, Nonduality. The identity of the apparently individualized soul with the Supreme Soul (Jivatman and Paramatman) is a subject that transcends all others, and which ennobles the aspiring mind like no other.

Taking Lord Gaudapada's famous commentary on the Mandukyopanisad, a series of classes will be engaged in that is designed to help the human mind, stuck in relativity and accustomed to duality, to penetrate into the supreme mysteries of nondual Reality. This indepth process, taken up in sacred retreat, will be further implemented via periods of deep meditation.

Location: Windwood Waters retreat site near Stevenson, WA
Arrival: Thursday, May 22, between 4:00 & 6:00 pm
Departure: Monday, May 26, 1:00pm
Registration: Starts now. Tuition and lodging fees are due by **May 16th**
Register by email: srvinfo@srv.org or by phone 808-990-3354
Costs: Tuition and meals: $410; Students:: $225 (lodging additional)
Lodging: private room single, $240; private room shared with 1 - 2 others, $160/person;
    semi-private lodge sleeping, $120*; Tenting, $80*   *bring your own bedding/towels

SRV American River Retreat over Independence Day
July 3 – 9, 2014, Forest Hill, CA
- *The Life and Teachings of Swami Vivekananda*

- Live in holy company for a full week – meditating, studying, serving, and growing together.
- Each morning begins with chanting from the Bhagavad Gita prior to meditation.
- Daily classes include essential teachings of Yoga and Vedanta,
- Afternoons include explorations and swimming/sunning along the American River
- Afternoon Chela Dharma class for teens and young adults
- Evening devotions at the altar, singing and chanting, meditation, and satsang.
- Concurrent Children's Retreat — Children, ages 6 to approximately 13 have their own simultaneous retreat. Activities include "salute to the sun," morning ritual, meditation, Vedic stories and lessons, and arts and crafts.

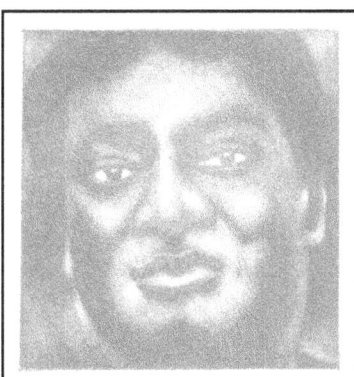

Location: Private land in Foresthill, California near the American River
Arrival: Arrive by 6pm, Thursday, July 3
Last day of retreat: Wednesday, July 9 (approximately noon, clean up follows)
Tuition: all inclusive
   Adults: $660 (full retreat) $275 (weekend, arrive Friday) $110/day
   Children/Students: $330 (full retreat) $140 (weekend, arrive Friday) $55/day
Registration: starts now and tuition is due by Monday, **June 23rd**
Financial hardship? Call 808-990-3354 to discuss options
Register by email: srvinfo@srv.org or by phone 808-990-3354

Navaratri Retreat on Lakshmi Puja
October 9 – 13, 2014, Stevenson, WA
Chanting and Study of the 108 Names of Sri Sarada Devi

Celebrating the subtle but palpable presence of the Wisdom Mother, SRV Associations offers their annual Navaratri retreat, held again at Windwood Waters on the Columbia River Gorge. Along with the chanting of the "108 Names of Sri Sarada," the devotees will take a deep look into the Mother scriptures of India, such as the Chandi and the Srimad Devi Bhagavatam.

Location: Windwood Waters retreat site near Stevenson Washington
Arrival: Thursday, October 9 after 4:00pm
Departure: Monday, October 13, 12:00pm (approximately)
Tuition & Meals: Adults: $410: Student:: $225 (lodging additional)
Lodging: Private room single, $240; Private room shared, $160/person
semi-private lodge sleeping, $120; tenting, $80 bring your own bedding/towels
Registration: Starts now. Tuition and other fees are due by **September 26th**

Plus:

Weekend Seminar on the Bhagavad Gita
July 26 – 27, 2014, SRV Oregon Ashram
Specific Gita Chapters & Slokas with Meditation

Location: SRV Oregon Ashram in Portland
Saturday, July 26: 6:00am – 5:00pm (breakfast/dinner)
Sunday, July 27: 6:00am – 5:00pm (breakfast only)
(2 class sessions each day. Gita chanted in the morning)

Tuition: $220; student, $110 Due by **July 18th**
Accommodations: This is a non-residential seminar
Contact us if you would like assistance with lodging.
808-990-3354 // srvinfo@srv.org

During this weekend seminar, the essential message of the Bhagavad Gita will be expounded.
As Sri Ramakrishna has stated, *"The essence of the Gita is what one gets when one repeats the word "gita" over and over again. It turns into "tyagi," which means renunciation....."*

A Blissful Confluence of Religious and Philosophical Wisdom from all Religions
The "In The Spirit" Interviews of Lex Hixon

From the early 1970's on through the late 1980's, Lex Hixon hosted a radio program in New York City that was unprecedented in its depth, scope, insight and unique creativity.

The fruit of this selfless work spans the spiritual, artistic and intellectual heart and mind of both Eastern and Western cultures. With subtle tenderness and insight, though never lacking the penetrating edge which makes for excellent broadcasting, Lex welcomed the orthodox and the unorthodox, the conservative and the radical, the famous and the obscure, the popular and the controversial, the powerful and the humble, the aggressive and the retiring.

Included in this copious series are inspirational interviews with gurus, yogis, swamis, priests, roshis, rabbis/rebbes, sheikhs, lamas, rinpoches, poets, musicians, psychics, occultists, authors, writers, teachers, politicians, businessmen and more.

Interviews with:
Dalai Lama
Mother Teresa
Sheikh Muzaffer
Shlomo Carlebach
Alan Watts
Swami Muktananda
Ram Das

Programs on:
Sri Ramakrishna
The Karmapa
Ramana Maharshi
Meister Ekhart
Sri Aurobindo
Padre Pio
Swami Vivekananda

"IN THE SPIRIT" Trio Sets *on cd or cassette*
Representing all the Major Religions hosted by Lex Hixon

Buddhist
B1 - Dalai Lama
Kalu Rinpoche
Trungpa Rinpoche

B2 - Eido Roshi
Soen Roshi
Maesumi Roshi

B3 - Phillip Kapleau
Bernie Glassman
Robert Thurman

Christianity
C1 - Mother Teresa
Padre Pio
Meister Ekhart

Islam/Sufism
IS1 - Sheikh Muzaffer
Guru Bawa
Sheikh Nur Al Jerrahi

Judaism
J1 - Rabbi Shlomo Carlebach
Rebbe Gedalia
Rabbi Zalman Schachter

J2 - Rebbe Meyer Fund
Rabbi Dovid Din
Rabbi Lynn Gottleib

Lex Hixon
H1 - On the Haj
On the Karmapa
On Himself

Professors & Authors
PA1 - Huston Smith
Christopher Isherwood
Jack Kornfield

PA2 - David Spangler
Alan Watts
Alan Ginsberg

Shamanism/Amer. Indian
SI1 - Oh Shinnah
Dhani Thorna
Don Juan

Vedic
V1 - Sri Ramakrishna

V2 - Vivekananda
Nikhilananda
Prabhavananda

V3 - Dayananda
Muktananda
Satchitananda

V4 - Ramana Maharshi
Sri Aurobindo
Krishnamurti

V5 - Meher Baba
Sri Chinmoy
Ram Das

V6 - Divine Mother
of the Universe

cd sets: $45 ea., cassette sets: $35 ea., individual: $10/tape, $15/cd plus shipping

from **SRV Associations**, PO Box 1364, Honokaa, HI 96727
Email orders: srvinfo@srv.org
Website: www.srv.org - Order form provided ▪ (808) 990-3354

Advaita-satya-amritam

NECTAR
of Non-Dual Truth

Donation/Order Form
Suggested donation $12 per issue

Nectar #30 is available for free if you write, email, or call for a copy by January 15, 2015. Your generous donations make Nectar available to others and help us to widen our distribution.

Those who donate $12 or more for the next issue, will be added to our subscriber's list.

- ❑ Please send me/my friend a free copy of the next issue of Nectar.
- ❑ Send me ___ copies to give to friends or a Spiritual Center of my choice.
- ❑ I am including the names of persons/centers I want to receive Nectar. *Fill out back of form.*
- ❑ I want to help SRV's Free Nectar Distribution Program ($50 and up)
- ❑ I want to help widen Nectar's Distribution ($200 and up)
- ❑ I want to make sure there are future issues of Nectar ($500 and up)

Please fill out the back side of this form and mail it with your check to:
SRV Associations, PO Box 1364, Honokaa, HI 96727
MasterCard or Visa accepted • Make checks payable to: SRV Associations
808-990-3354 • srvinfo@srv.org • www.srv.org

#29

Advaita-satya-amritam

NECTAR
of Non-Dual Truth

Donation/Order Form
Suggested donation $12 per issue

Nectar #30 is available for free if you write, email, or call for a copy by January 15, 2015. Your generous donations make Nectar available to others and help us to widen our distribution.

Those who donate $12 or more for the next issue, will be added to our subscriber's list.

- ❑ Please send me/my friend a free copy of the next issue of Nectar.
- ❑ Send me ___ copies to give to friends or a Spiritual Center of my choice.
- ❑ I am including the names of persons/centers I want to receive Nectar. *Fill out back of form.*
- ❑ I want to help SRV's Free Nectar Distribution Program ($50 and up)
- ❑ I want to help widen Nectar's Distribution ($200 and up)
- ❑ I want to make sure there are future issues of Nectar ($500 and up)

Please fill out the back side of this form and mail it with your check to:
SRV Associations, PO Box 1364, Honokaa, HI 96727
MasterCard or Visa accepted • Make checks payable to: SRV Associations
808-990-3354 • srvinfo@srv.org • www.srv.org

#29

Advaita-satya-amritam

NECTAR
of Non-Dual Truth

Donation/Order Form
Suggested donation $12 per issue

Nectar #30 is available for free if you write, email, or call for a copy by January 15, 2015. Your generous donations make Nectar available to others and help us to widen our distribution.

Those who donate $12 or more for the next issue, will be added to our subscriber's list.

- ❑ Please send me/my friend a free copy of the next issue of Nectar.
- ❑ Send me ___ copies to give to friends or a Spiritual Center of my choice.
- ❑ I am including the names of persons/centers I want to receive Nectar. *Fill out back of form.*
- ❑ I want to help SRV's Free Nectar Distribution Program ($50 and up)
- ❑ I want to help widen Nectar's Distribution ($200 and up)
- ❑ I want to make sure there are future issues of Nectar ($500 and up)

Please fill out the back side of this form and mail it with your check to:
SRV Associations, PO Box 1364, Honokaa, HI 96727
MasterCard or Visa accepted • Make checks payable to: SRV Associations
808-990-3354 • srvinfo@srv.org • www.srv.org

#29

Your Information:

Name: _____
Address: _____
City, State, Zip: _____
Email: _____

Additional Address: (please use a sheet of paper for more addresses)

Name: _____
Address: _____
City, State, Zip: _____
Email: _____

Do you wish to pay by Mastercard or Visa?
Card No.: _____
Exp. date: _____ **Phone no.:** _____
Signature: _____

Questions? call SRV Associations: 808-990-3354

Your Information:

Name: _____
Address: _____
City, State, Zip: _____
Email: _____

Additional Address: (please use a sheet of paper for more addresses)

Name: _____
Address: _____
City, State, Zip: _____
Email: _____

Do you wish to pay by Mastercard or Visa?
Card No.: _____
Exp. date: _____ **Phone no.:** _____
Signature: _____

Questions? call SRV Associations: 808-990-3354

Your Information:

Name: _____
Address: _____
City, State, Zip: _____
Email: _____

Additional Address: (please use a sheet of paper for more addresses)

Name: _____
Address: _____
City, State, Zip: _____
Email: _____

Do you wish to pay by Mastercard or Visa?
Card No.: _____
Exp. date: _____ **Phone no.:** _____
Signature: _____

Questions? call SRV Associations: 808-990-3354

www.ingramcontent.com/pod-product-compliance
Lightning Source LLC
Chambersburg PA
CBHW081127080526
44587CB00021B/3774